THE PREDICAMENT

Does it make sense—can it make sense—for someone who appreciates the explanatory power of modern science to continue believing in a traditional religious account of the ultimate nature and purpose of our universe? This book is intended for those who care about that question and are dissatisfied with the rigid dichotomies that dominate the contemporary debate. The extremists won't be interested—those who assume that science answers all the questions that matter, and those so certain of their religious faith that dialogue with science, philosophy, or other faith traditions seems unnecessary. But far more people today recognize that matters of faith are complex, that doubt is endemic to belief, and that dialogue is indispensable in our day.

In eight probing chapters, the authors of *The Predicament of Belief* consider the most urgent reasons for doubting that religious claims—in particular, those embedded in the Christian tradition—are likely to be true. They develop a version of Christian faith that preserves the tradition's core insights but also gauges the varying degrees of certainty with which those insights can still be affirmed. Along the way, they address such questions as the ultimate origin of the universe, the existence of innocent suffering, the challenge of religious plurality, and how to understand the extraordinary claim that an ancient teacher rose from the dead. They end with a discussion of what their conclusions imply about the present state and future structure of churches and other communities in which Christian affirmations are made.

Philip Clayton is Dean of the Faculty at Claremont School of Theology and Provost of Claremont Lincoln University. He is author or editor of twenty-two books and close to two hundred articles in philosophy, theology, and the religion-science debate.

Steven Knapp is the sixteenth president of the George Washington University in Washington, DC, where he is also a professor of English. He is the author of two books and author or co-author of numerous articles and lectures on literature, literary theory, philosophy, and religion.

THE PREDICAMENT OF BELIEF

SCIENCE, PHILOSOPHY, FAITH

PHILIP CLAYTON

and

STEVEN KNAPP

OXFORD

UNIVERSITY PRESS

OXFORD
UNIVERSITY PRESS

Great Clarendon Street, Oxford, OX2 6DP,
United Kingdom

Oxford University Press is a department of the University of Oxford.
It furthers the University's objective of excellence in research, scholarship,
and education by publishing worldwide. Oxford is a registered trade mark of
Oxford University Press in the UK and in certain other countries

The moral rights of the author have been asserted

First published 2011
First published in paperback 2013

Impression: 1

British Library Cataloguing in Publication Data
Data available

Library of Congress Cataloging in Publication Data
Data available

ISBN 978-0-19-969527-0 (Hbk.)
978-0-19-967796-2 (Pbk.)

Printed by the MPG Printgroup, UK

Contents

Preface

This is a difficult era for those who find themselves committed to the values of scientific rationality and yet moved by the claims of a religious tradition. It is rare for such persons to receive a hearing, let alone an enthusiastic one, from either the scientifically minded or the religiously committed. Formerly open camps have circled the wagons, and exploratory dialogue has given way to *ad hominem* rhetoric. Not surprisingly in such a climate, it is not easy for inquiring readers to find resources that will help them determine how far the assumptions of science, together with other sources of religious doubt, really do cut into the viability of religious claims. As a result, it is hard to decide what parts of one's tradition it makes sense to reject or retain.

To look with probing, even skeptical eyes at religious belief is not, after all, a normal part of the work of religious scholars, at least not in our day. In an era of increasingly open hostility toward religious truth claims, some of it voiced by distinguished scientists, it has become almost exclusively the task of secular philosophers and other opponents of religion to raise the probing questions. In response, religious scholars are inclined more and more to take a defensive posture, focusing their efforts on protecting religion in general, or more often the specific beliefs of their own tradition, from attack. In an era of such antipathy toward religious truth claims—so the reasoning appears to go—scholars who are in any way sympathetic to religion should concentrate exclusively on its defense, lest they inadvertently give ammunition to its opponents.

As understandable as this response may be, it has produced a literature unhelpfully confined to rhetorical combat. Those who eschew both sides have usually become agnostics, abjuring the debate in favor of spiritual practices, religious ethics, or a mystical "unknowing" in the face of questions of ultimacy. Best-seller lists are packed with hostile treatments of religious belief bearing titles such as *The God Delusion*,

God is Not Great, Breaking the Spell, and *Religion Explained*; they in turn have spawned dozens of religious counterattacks. But remarkably rare are the treatments that, while basically sympathetic to religious belief, attempt to sift carefully through the arguments for and against core religious propositions such as the existence of God. Precisely this lack in the contemporary literature provides the motivation of this book.

Now there might seem to be a glaring error in the claim just made. Is the market not full of books that criticize religious traditions from within and advocate revising them in ways that will make them more relevant to the world we now live in? Such books have subjected Christian, Jewish, and, more recently, Muslim belief and practice to piercing scrutiny. They typically argue that much (and many argue that virtually all) of what these traditions once held is no longer plausible. At first glance, it would seem that these books sufficiently fill the need for self-critical treatments of religious belief.

As a rule, however, the revisionists perform only *half* the required task. Among those interested in the Christian tradition, for example, the revisionist or "liberal" authors are frankly critical of inherited doctrines, cheerfully jettisoning convictions that once defined the core commitments of Christianity. And yet many authors subject their own proposals to rather less critical attention (although there are some notable exceptions).[1] Whatever is deemed worthy of pre-serving—an experience of "new being," a commitment to environ-mental stewardship, or resistance to racial, sexual, or economic oppression—is often put forward with the same unwavering passion of religious conviction with which the traditional beliefs themselves were once advanced. More to the immediate point: less critical scru-tiny is focused on the assumptions that lead these authors to reject the religious truth claims their own proposals are intended to replace.

In all the respects we have just mentioned, commentary on religion typically stops short, at present, of addressing what we are calling the predicament of religious belief in today's world. That predicament, as we understand it, has two facets: on one side, the difficulty of for-mulating traditional claims about what is ultimately the case in ways that take full account of all the reasons for doubting those claims; on the other side, the need to do justice to the axiological and theoretical power of those accounts of ultimate reality that metaphysical reflection and religious traditions variously suggest.

We begin this book with the first of those two aspects, that is, with reasons for doubt—more precisely, with the reasons we take to be the most serious ones for doubting either religious claims in general or Christian claims in particular. The grounds for doubt that are introduced in Chapter I represent, in our judgment, deep and serious challenges. These are the kinds of worries that give or *should* give serious pause to people who are wondering whether Christian belief—the case on which we will mainly focus—is still viable. Moreover, it seems to us that theologians who work professionally at formulating religious teachings have an obligation to understand and respond to these grounds for doubt. It may well be the case that belief in God, at least in its Christian form, should not continue unchanged in the face of these critical concerns.

Yet we are not convinced that these worries by themselves are sufficient to render every belief in some form of ultimate reality outdated or irrational. Over the course of a research program lasting more than two decades now, in numerous conference publications, and in a variety of articles and books, we have sought to determine what revisions were required by the challenges to belief and what responses remained available in the face of those challenges. When it comes to the more specific claims of the Christian tradition, one must acknowledge the specific assumptions, commitments, and experiences that motivate an ongoing interest in this tradition and its particular affirmations. *Given* this set of interests, we will show, some traditional claims remain problematic, some have an indeterminate status, and some are in fact untouched by the standard criticisms. Even in the case of Christianity's most contentious claims, those regarding the ultimate fate and status of its founder, it turns out that there is a relatively small number of serious objections and a limited number of ways of responding to them. When one gives these matters sustained critical attention, resisting the tendency toward snap judgments in one direction or another, it is possible to develop a pretty good sense of the lay of the land.

We are under no illusion, however, that the arguments presented in this book are likely to sway those in either of the warring camps mentioned at the outset. There is no way, for instance, to compel a physicist who regards the universe as simply the meaningless result of mindless forces to take seriously—or to regard with any interest at all—the degree to which the very ability of human beings to understand such phenomena raises questions that point beyond what physics itself can establish. We cannot deny the immense emotional appeal of restricting one's view of reality to whatever can be measured and explained by the lights of one's own discipline! Similarly, there is no way to compel a contented believer in traditional religious claims to take seriously the grounds for wondering if those claims are actually true. Our arguments are not aimed at those who are happy to remain at either extreme, but are offered as guidance for those who wish to go where reason and experience may lead. We dedicate this effort to all, of every faith or no faith, who approach the ultimate reality in that spirit.

This book is the result of discussions that occurred over a period of nearly 25 years. We cannot hope to do justice to all the teachers, colleagues, students, and friends whose suggestions, criticisms, confirmations, and corrections have helped to shape our argument (whether or not they would in any way agree with its final form).

Three readers – the anonymous reviewers for Oxford University Press – offered suggestions that led to a major revision of the book as a whole. But we owe a large debt to many others, including John Cobb, Jr., Louis Dupré, Kate Clayton, Dorothy Hale, Stuart Kauffman, Catherine Keller, Jeffrey Knapp, Jesse Knapp, Robert McKenzie, Walter Benn Michaels, Jürgen Moltmann, Wolfhart Pannenberg, Alvin Plantinga, Owen Thomas, Kevin Vanhoozer, Wesley Wildman, Nicholas Wolterstorff, and several who have passed from this veil of tears: William Alston, Donald Davidson, and Bernard Williams. Justin Heinzekehr did invaluable work preparing the index and checking references.

But our largest debt of gratitude is to our families, who graciously accommodated, over a quarter century, an endless stream of telephone calls and weekend conversations. To them we can only say, in the words of Mahatma Gandhi, that 'forgiveness is the attribute of the strong'.

I

Reasons for doubt

The modern predicament

What is ultimately the case? Is there a source of all that is, and is there a direction in which everything is tending? Are the source and goal the same; is there a single reality that encompasses them both? And if so, does that reality have anything to do with us, with the way we live and the things we say and do here, in the brief time we spend on a minuscule fragment of the totality of everything there is?

These questions, or ones like them, have preoccupied large numbers of human beings since the dawn of civilization, and perhaps far longer. Over the course of human history, countless answers to these questions—call them, for short, *questions of ultimacy*—have been offered. In fact, whatever their differences may be in other respects, one of the features shared by all human societies of any duration has been their tendency to formulate questions of ultimacy and to attempt to answer them. Claims, theories, beliefs about what is ultimately the case and what they mean for human existence are among the salient artifacts of all human cultures.

At the same time that we recognize the depth and power of the ancient traditions, however, our explorations of these questions today must take place in light of new challenges. Contemporary grounds for doubting the traditional answers are serious enough that one may well wonder whether the questions can be answered at all and, indeed, whether it is even still meaningful to pose them, at least in the manner in which they were formulated by the great traditions of religious faith and reflection.

In responding to these worries, one has to start somewhere, and we take as our starting point the claims embodied in one traditional way of answering questions about what is ultimately the case, the one broadly known as "Christian." Beneath all the layers of historical and cultural detail that define its multiple branches, the Christian tradition rests upon a provocative hypothesis about the nature of the universe and its ultimate source. That hypothesis can be restated as the belief or wager that behind or beyond all things, at the beginning of everything we see and know, there exists an ultimate reality that in some sense intended us (or beings like us) to be here and—again in *some* sense—desires our flourishing. Moreover, that ultimate reality has actually conveyed its intentions to human beings, whether directly or indirectly, and has done so in part through its extraordinary involvement in a particular set of events in human history.

Many books have been written about the "modern predicament" and the threat it poses to the traditional ways of conceiving and responding to the questions of ultimacy—and most of all to those religious beliefs that depend on claims about miraculous events said to have happened in the very distant past.[1] All three of the "Abrahamic" traditions (so called because they all give a major founding role to a single ancient patriarch) are often said to fit that description. One of them, however—the Christian one—is unusual in the amount of weight it places on a single, relatively brief episode, about which it makes perhaps the most extraordinary claims of any of these three traditions.

Modernity (not to mention postmodernity!) is often taken to have changed the nature of human thought and human culture so radically that ancient beliefs are no longer viable, simply because they belong to a pre-modern era. Responding to this charge, numerous books written to defend Christianity against the various threats posed by modernity argue that things have not changed as much as might appear. Others argue that the changes are real but illegitimate and so should be rejected by those who hold to the true faith. Still others suggest that the changes are vast and legitimate but do not affect the core beliefs on which the religion depends; or, finally, that we can save the core beliefs by reinterpreting them, giving them a modern or postmodern interpretation that will enable them to thrive in this no-longer-new intellectual environment.[2]

A great deal of excellent thought and eloquent writing has gone into the project of extricating Christianity from the modern predicament by means of one or more of these strategies. We do not wish to minimize that effort or those achievements, let alone to claim that our approach is a radical departure from those of our predecessors. We have learned from these defenders of traditional Christian belief (as well as of defenders of other faiths and of religion more generally) and draw frequently on their arguments in what follows. But we do diverge in important ways from those who maintain that the threat to Christian belief and commitment emanates merely from a cultural change in the way human beings understand themselves and what surrounds them. We belong to a growing body of people who are committed, or at least strongly drawn, to the ancient claims but who are also deeply struck by evidence and arguments that point in the opposite direction. We respect those for whom the traditional Christian claims seem to need no defense or who believe that the objections can be easily answered by the various forms of Christian apologetics. But it seems to us, as it does to many others, scholars and laypeople alike, that there are strong and sometimes compelling reasons for doubting whether some of the traditional Christian claims are actually true. Many of these reasons would not have arisen without the changes that are part of modernity—for instance, the rise of modern natural science. Others are themselves quite ancient and would likely have emerged (or reemerged) in the course of human reflection, with or without the aid of science or other peculiarly modern developments. What is new in their case is not the reasons themselves so much as the freedom and safety in which they can now be discussed, thanks to the rise of modern ideas like tolerance and freedom of conscience that were either absent or suppressed until the last three centuries (and that are still resisted, sometimes violently, in many parts of the world).

There is another dimension of the modern predicament besides the reasons for doubt we will survey in a moment. Starting as far back as the seventeenth century, there has been a widening gap between, on one side, discourse about the ultimate nature of the universe and the truth or falsity of religious claims in general and, on the other side, discourse about the highly specific claims that emerge from the testimony and experience of particular religious traditions. The former is generally perceived as rational, dispassionate, and, increasingly, the purview of academic specialists; the latter as personal and passionate, more a matter of autobiography than of inquiry. Some even doubt that the claims of a particular tradition should be regarded as truth claims at all, interpreting them instead as vehicles of ethical and emotional engagement.

We will return to the question of what this gap between general and particular actually involves. Meanwhile, one does not need to be a specialist to recognize the contrast between general philosophical arguments about the nature of God and highly specific claims about a particular historical figure like Jesus of Nazareth, such as the claim that he was raised from the dead. Indeed, one of the central tasks of this book will be to underscore the sharp contrast between these two types of claims and to offer a convincing account of their relationship. In order to set up that task, however, we begin by spelling out, in this opening chapter, the most compelling reasons for doubting that the central claims of Christianity are actually true. Our list of these reasons for doubt is not meant to be shocking, original, or ingenious. On the contrary, we have sought to identify what scholars and nonscholars alike will recognize as a list of the considerations that cause thoughtful people to doubt some of the central Christian claims. In the remainder of the book we will offer a series of arguments aimed at showing at least some of the ways—not the only but the most compelling ways we have been able to identify—in which these considerations can be answered.

For reasons that will emerge over the course of the succeeding chapters, we remain committed to the core Christian hypothesis, despite all the sources of doubt. But we must emphasize from the start that there are many ways of defending such a commitment that are, in our view, problematic. For instance, some make the argument that faith should step in wherever reason fails.[3] Others appeal to religious feeling or religious "experience" as something that is both more elusive and more fundamental than anything one can reason about. Still others appeal to the richness of Christian "symbols" as sufficient to motivate Christian practice, despite the multiple ways in which such symbols can be understood.[4] Another response is that of Christian agnostics, who are content to act on Christian claims while eschewing both the possibility and the need to determine if any of those claims is actually true.

Our approach is different from all these responses, and that for at least one major reason. What all such approaches have in common is their tendency, intentional or not, to *immunize* Christian claims from the criticisms of non-Christians. (In fact, they are often used to immunize beliefs from criticism by other Christians as well, such as those who think that one of the most important of all Christian values is fidelity to the truth and who therefore worry—rightly, in our view—about the dangers of being misled by delusion or error.) To put it bluntly (again, without impugning motives), many of the typical responses amount to what might be called *immunization strategies*.[5]

For those who reject such strategies and yet still want to know whether the Christian understanding of ultimate reality is viable, there is only one alternative, and that is *to understand the reasons for doubt as fully and clearly as possible*: to look those reasons, so to speak, directly in the eye. Only then can one decide whether or not there are countervailing reasons that rightly override the reasons for doubt. And only after these reasons have been presented can one determine how much doubt appropriately remains, and what to do in response. Some critics will object that we have not gone nearly far enough in our response to the predicament of Christian belief today, whereas others will complain that we have gone far too far. It is good to keep in mind, however, that those who seriously engage the arguments share at least that much common ground, in contrast to the kinds of strategies mentioned in the preceding paragraph.

This, at any rate, is the task we undertake in the following pages. But first, it is important to state what many take to be the main reasons for doubting that the core Christian understanding of ultimacy can emerge intact from its modern predicament.

(i) Science

For reasons not hard to understand, the rise of experimental science presents a reason—perhaps the single most important one—for doubting Christian clams. Over the course of roughly the last three centuries, the modern era has been deeply influenced by scientific methods, results, and ways of thinking. Scarcely a week passes nowadays without the announcement of some major or at least significant breakthrough in the ability of human beings to explain the world around them, or the stars beyond them, or the inner workings of their own bodies. These were all mysteries for most of the generations of human existence. But now many believe it is only a matter of time before all such mysteries yield to the inevitable advance of science, which professes to identify their natural causes without the need to imagine any reality beyond the one whose ultimate description is provided by the laws of physics.

Consider the stunning advances of science in the last few decades alone. The WMAP and Hubble Space Telescopes, supplemented by ground-based instruments of extreme sophistication, provide more and more evidence that the universe looks exactly the way it should look according to the so-called Big Bang theory of its origin. In very recent memory, biologists succeeded in decoding the human genome, enlisting the aid of computers to read the fundamental chemical instructions that tell our cells (via protein formation) how to produce all the intricate structures of our bodies and how to carry out cellular processes. One part of our bodies—the human brain—is indeed so intricate that we are just now beginning to develop imaging technologies sufficient to allow scientists to reconstruct the causal processes behind brain functions and dysfunctions. The task is daunting, but many scientists believe that within a few decades we will understand the causal mechanisms that produce human consciousness, thought, and feeling. (In Chapter 3 we offer some reasons for doubting this particular claim.)

Our ancestors found, in the plants around them, surprising cures for a wide range of human ailments, but they had no idea what it was in the plants that had the power to cure. Now we know, at least in general terms, how the chemicals in a plant interact with those in our bodies, and we are constantly refining our understanding of the mechanisms that connect natural and synthetic chemicals to their particular therapeutic effects. As medical knowledge has advanced, it has vindicated much of the lore of traditional medicine, but only by explaining traditional medical effects in ways that the original practitioners could not have grasped.

The upshot of all these discoveries is that the natural world—that is, the universe as explained in terms of the laws discovered by the natural sciences—increasingly looks like a completely closed and self-explanatory system. In fact, the progress of science today depends on the willingness of scientists to assume that whatever needs explaining will yield, sooner or later, to naturalistic explanations—which, again, means explanations given in terms of regular cause-and-effect relations among things in this world, without any influence or interference from anything beyond this world. That essential working assumption to which all scientists must subscribe (at least as long as they are working as scientists) is sometimes called the *presumption of naturalism.*

Some philosophers—notably David Hume, the great eighteenth-century British skeptic—have maintained that the presumption of naturalism rules out the possibility that *anything* that happens in our universe is the result of an action emanating from outside that universe.[6] To be precise, Hume did not quite deny that a supernatural power might exist outside the universe, or that such a power might bring about an event in our universe that otherwise would not have occurred. Instead, he argued that we could never have *sufficient reason* to assume that something supernatural had happened, because it would always be more rational to explain anything that occurred in our universe in terms of causes arising within that universe itself. In other words, Hume realized that what we are calling the presumption of naturalism was a *methodological presumption,* a rule governing how we ought to think about what happens in our universe; not a *metaphysical law,* which would govern what might possibly occur, whether we could ever know that it had occurred or not.

It is important to recognize that the presumption of naturalism is methodological not metaphysical, because otherwise the presumption would be arbitrary, a matter of (nonreligious) faith or dogma. No matter how successful science has been or ever will be, it has not disproved, and in principle never can disprove, the possibility that what Hume called a "miracle"—an event brought about by the intervention of a supernatural power—might actually occur. Hume was extremely helpful, to religious and nonreligious thinkers alike, in clarifying the difference between what *can* happen and what we human observers *have reason to think* has happened.

But some religious thinkers overestimate, in our opinion, the importance of the distinction between the methodological and the metaphysical versions of a presumption of naturalism. They jump from the recognition that science cannot rule out the possibility of miracles to the conclusion that science leaves a traditional belief in miracles untouched. And that, in our judgment, is a mistake. It underestimates the effect of scientific successes on the traditional tendency to suppose, when something extraordinary happens, that it must have been the result of a supernatural intervention. It is also a mistake because it prevents those who accept it from asking themselves why the universe should be such that it lends itself so readily to scientific explanation. In the next chapter, we will take up that very question. We will ask why the ultimate reality might be such that a universe would exist with the sorts of lawlike patterns that are so powerfully suited to scientific explanation. Meanwhile, we register the success of scientific explanation as one of the main reasons, perhaps even the most important reason, that many people no longer feel compelled to explain their existence in terms of an ultimate reality that is greater, more perfect, or in the long run more important than the reality they encounter in their ordinary finite and mortal existence.

(ii) Evil

The best-known, and surely the most troubling and painful, problem for the credibility of Christian claims is the one traditionally known as the problem of evil. Stated in its simplest terms, this is the problem of reconciling the hypothesis of a good and powerful God with the existence of bad things that such a God, if this being really existed, would be expected to stop or prevent.

This reason for doubt is no less serious, intellectually, than the other reasons. But it also has an emotional force that other objections to Christian claims—and indeed to theistic claims more generally—cannot match. Consider:

- One night, in the dark, a village in Colombia is covered by a sudden mudslide that claims the lives of all but a handful of its inhabitants. (The fact that many of those inhabitants are devout Christians has no apparent effect on their fate.) If events in this world are ultimately under the control of a benevolent supernatural being, what could have prevented that being from either stabilizing the hillside or, if for some reason that wasn't possible, at least warning the villagers of the impending slide? Similar questions were raised, on a much larger scale, by the Indian Ocean tsunami that killed more than a quarter of a million people in just a few hours in December 2004, and by the January 2010 Haitian earthquake that may have killed many more (see Chapter 3).

- A promising young girl in Baltimore is found dead after months of starvation and torture by her deranged foster mother. Many people—her teachers, the neighbors, the social worker responsible for her case—were in a position to wonder why the girl was missing for so many weeks, but none took the trouble to find out why she was absent from school or otherwise unavailable. Even the slightest imaginable pressure from a benevolent God would presumably have sufficed to kindle their interest, but apparently this did not occur.

- A rebel army in eastern Africa fills its ranks by kidnapping children between the ages of 8 and 16 and then compels them to commit acts of unimaginable violence or, in the case of some children, makes them the sexual slaves of the rebel commanders. Again, no sign of divine intervention.

Tales of natural and human horror could be multiplied a thousand fold. And yet even these three examples are sufficient to highlight the obvious problem: our experience very often presents us with the opposite of what we would expect from a benevolent creator who had the ability to prevent such things from occurring. So far we have not even mentioned the event that probably plays a greater role than any other in the thinking of modern theologians who wrestle with the problem of evil: the Nazi Holocaust, in which, only a few short decades ago, one of the most intellectually and technologically advanced of all historically Christian societies undertook the systematic destruction of an entire people. Obviously, anyone who wishes to argue that the reasons for Christian commitment override the reasons for doubt must give some account of why it is possible, in a God-created universe, for events like these to occur.

The problem of evil is not unrelated to another question, one that goes to the heart of supposing that the ultimate reality is the kind of being that (or who) would or could take any sort of interest in the welfare of human beings. Even if we have reason to think that there is a mind-like or (in some sense) a personal being at the beginning and end of all reality, why should we suppose that what matters to such a being—so much vaster and more powerful than anything we can concretely understand or imagine—is anything even remotely resembling what matters to us?

(iii) Religious plurality

In many ways, this is the most obvious, and one of the most ancient, of all reasons for doubting the claims of Christianity: other traditions make equally strong claims about the nature and purposes of the ultimate reality, and their adherents are at least as strongly committed to them as Christians are to theirs. The challenge of religious plurality does not lie simply in the fact that there are many religions. Instead, it lies in the fact that there are many religions that command the allegiance of vast portions of humanity; that give rise to truly impressive personalities (prophets, saints, gurus, as well as believers of ordinary station but impressive moral and spiritual strength); and that provide the basis for extraordinary achievements in the arts, in individual moral behavior, and in social reform.[7]

There are several reasons why the existence of multiple religions, each possessing the cultural and moral power just mentioned, creates a problem for the credibility of Christian claims. First, there is the obvious question: if other people believe other things with equal conviction and, as far as we can tell, with equally good spiritual and moral effects, what makes anyone think that her religion is preferable to theirs? Indeed, is any one of the major world religions more likely to be true than any of the others? How does one know that one's commitment to Christianity is not just the accidental result of one's having been born and raised in a particular culture, a particular time and place, or indeed a particular family?

There is another, perhaps less obvious, reason why the fact of religious plurality is a source of doubt, a reason that connects the issue of religious plurality with the problem of evil. The fact of religious plurality compels us to ask why, if Christian claims are true, multiple religions should exist in the first place. For if Christian claims are true, then, at a minimum, the universe is grounded in an ultimate, and ultimately benevolent, reality that in some sense seeks communion with those finite creatures who are capable of entering into such communion. A reality that seeks communion must be in some sense a *personal* reality, that is, a reality capable of having desires and purposes and acting in accordance with them. Why should it be so hard for the personal being who is the ground and therefore the creator of our universe—if there is such a being—to communicate its intentions in a relatively coherent and uniform way, at least to those of its creatures who are open to receive them?

We must mention one last reason for those interested in the possible viability of Christian claims to worry about the plurality of religions, this one more intimately related to the history of Christianity itself.

There is one "other religion" in particular with which Christianity has wrestled since its inception, with consequences that have called into question not only its intellectual credibility but its moral value. We have in mind the terrible history of Christian attitudes and actions toward the religion from which it originally emerged and without which its very existence is inconceivable. The unresolved tragedy of Christian relations with Judaism brings home, as strongly as anything does, the difficulty of claiming the superiority of Christian affirmations over those of its religious alternatives.[8]

(iv) The state of the historical evidence

In provoking this set of urgent questions—why did God not prevent confusion and conflict by giving us all the same religion, and how could Christianity have turned so violently against the culture and traditions that gave it birth—the problem of religious plurality shades into another, though perhaps more subtle, question about traditional Christian claims. This challenge is raised by the Christian claim that God has acted to communicate God's nature and purposes with humanity in a uniquely clear and powerful way in the events associated with the life and death of a certain Jewish teacher or rabbi in the ancient Roman province of Palestine.

The records we have of the way that rabbi was remembered and understood by his followers do not show any obvious signs that supernatural care was taken to ensure their clarity. According to most experts, none of the records that has come down to us was directly produced by anyone who actually knew the rabbi, Jesus of Nazareth, during his earthly life. And the records themselves differ in striking ways both in the events they recount and the interpretations they place on those events. Three of those records, the Gospels according to Matthew, Mark, and Luke, are called the "Synoptic Gospels" because the structures of their narratives are similar enough that they can be printed in parallel columns, enabling a reader to see them together in a single glance (*syn* + *opsis*) and thus to compare their treatments of particular episodes or sayings in Jesus' life. But even those three Gospels—let alone the fourth, the Gospel According to John, which orders events in starkly different ways from the other three—disagree sharply among themselves.

To take just a single instance: they differ even over the question of who was present at Jesus' execution, what was said by Jesus and those around him, and what happened immediately afterwards. In Mark's account, his disciples all abandon Jesus before his execution, with only a few women remaining behind to watch "from a distance." Jesus says nothing to the two thieves who are crucified on his right and his left and who join the crowd in taunting him; in fact, he is quoted only as reciting the opening verse of Psalm 22 (which his hearers misunderstand); then he gives a loud cry, and the curtain of the great Jerusalem temple is torn in two. A centurion (the Roman officer presumably in charge of the execution squad) confesses, "Truly this man was God's son." Matthew's account is similar, except that, when Jesus dies, not only is the temple curtain torn in two; the earth shakes, the rocks are split, and the tombs of "the saints" are opened.

Luke's account is very different. This time, Jesus is not reported as having quoted the apparently despairing line from Psalm 22—"My God, my God, why have you forsaken me?" Instead he is quoted as asking God to forgive his executioners, and then as engaging in a rather extended dialogue with the two thieves, one of whom acknowledges Jesus' innocence and receives in return a promise of entry into Paradise. At the point of death, Jesus does not merely cry out with a loud voice, as in Mark and Matthew, but commends his spirit into the hands of God. When he dies, the temple curtain is split, as in Mark and Matthew, but there is no mention, as in Matthew, of an earthquake or an opening of tombs.

If we now turn to John—not one of the Synoptics, but arguably the most theologically influential of all four Gospels—the situation is even more strikingly different. This time, a group of Jesus' followers is depicted as actually present at the foot of his cross: the "beloved disciple" and several women, including Jesus' mother. Jesus does not address the thieves, but he does speak to his mother and the disciple, instructing them henceforth to regard each other as mother and son. After that, knowing that "all was now finished," Jesus says, "I am thirsty," is given a sponge dipped in vinegar, and then says, "It is finished." One of the soldiers pierces his side with a spear, an event that has no parallel in the other three Gospels. Finally, there is no mention of the temple curtain or the awestruck centurion, let alone of an earthquake or graves breaking open.

We have focused on the Gospel accounts of Jesus' death both because of their importance to all later Christian thought and because this is the one place in the story where all four Gospels most nearly agree; and yet they disagree to some extent on nearly every detail! Given the evidence these accounts collectively provide, we can't say whether any of Jesus' disciples was present or not; what Jesus said or didn't say; or what miraculous events did or did not occur upon the moment of his death. But disagreements among the New Testament accounts of Jesus' life are not the only reason for doubt that emanates from the state of the historical evidence. There is also the fact—in our view even more important—that all four Gospels, and all the writings that make up the rest of the New Testament corpus, were selected and preserved by people with a strong vested interest in how these events would be remembered and interpreted.

There is a crucial concept in criminal law known as the "chain of custody." This refers to the importance of ensuring that, when evidence is found at a crime scene, a careful record be kept of all the hands through which that evidence passes before it reaches the trial. Otherwise there is simply no way to be certain that the evidence has not been altered by those with a vested interest in the outcome. Well, when it comes to evidence about the life and death and teachings and actions of Jesus of Nazareth, there is nothing remotely resembling a chain of custody. Most scholars think the Gospels themselves were written decades after the events they recount, so there is no way of knowing to what extent the evidence they contain was sifted and sorted, refined or embellished, before they achieved their final written form. Even after that process, still more decades passed before the creation of the earliest manuscripts of these writings that we possess, and all the while the texts on which those manuscripts were based were entirely in the control of people with a vested interest, once again, in how Jesus would be remembered and understood.[9] Indeed, according to many recent scholars, particularly those informed by feminist theory and historiography, accounts of Jesus' words and actions show signs of having been reshaped in many ways by the ideological biases of generations of authors and redactors.[10]

This complex picture has been complicated still further by the discovery, as recently as the middle of the last century, that the Gospels as we know them were carefully selected from a much larger body of writings about Jesus, writings that the early Christian church deliberately suppressed and that were therefore buried, literally, for millennia before their accidental reemergence.[11] Scholars continue to debate whether material in the so-called Gnostic gospels is just as ancient as the material in the canonical Gospels, that is, the ones accepted as authoritative by the vast majority of Christians ever since. But the fact undeniably remains that some accounts were carefully preserved while others were either accidentally neglected or deliberately suppressed, and it is hard to imagine a stronger reason for questioning the "chain of custody" than that!

Of course, all of our evidence about events and personalities in the ancient world is problematic to some extent, largely because it is so dependent on the accidents of preservation, which in turn depend so heavily on who were the victors in ancient conflicts and therefore had the power to determine what was saved or destroyed or allowed to disappear. The complexity and uncertainty of the historical record of Jesus' life and teachings would not matter so much if those records did not contain such truly extraordinary claims about the world-historical, and indeed the cosmic, importance of this single person. Jesus, they claim, was not just a charismatic religious teacher, who spoke in brilliant parables, challenged the religious authorities of his day, and inspired undying loyalty on the part of his disciples. Jesus was also, they claim, a miraculous healer, who spoke with the authority of the ultimate reality itself! In support of such unprecedented and, by their nature, hard-to-believe claims, we would seem to require even better evidence—and an even stronger "chain of custody"—than we would to support belief in, say, a dramatic but otherwise unremarkable (because perfectly natural) event like the assassination of a powerful ruler.

To summarize the various parts of this complex reason for doubting Christian claims: (1) it is hard enough to believe that not only the history but the cosmic destiny of humankind turned on the life and death of a single human being. But now add to that difficulty the facts (2) that this claim is embodied in a set of ancient writings that, in the earliest versions we possess, were produced decades after the events in question; (3) that those writings were created and then selected and preserved not by neutral scholars but by communities with a profound interest in how the events were to be remembered and interpreted; (4) that long-suppressed but recently discovered texts of equal or nearly equal antiquity (the so-called Gnostic gospels) present a very different picture of this person and his teachings from what we find in the canonical Gospels; and finally (5) that there are significant differences even among the canonical Gospels themselves, suggesting that each was shaped by the selective memory of a particular community and/or the preconceptions of its author or authors. Taken separately or together, these considerations are surely sufficient to raise doubts about the reliability of the historical testimony on which Christian claims about Jesus are founded.

(v) The claim of resurrection

There is one traditional Christian claim that requires particular attention, because it is so well known among nonbelievers and believers alike, so central to a nearly universal understanding of what Christianity is, and by its very nature so immediately and enormously dubious. This is the claim that, three days after his execution, Jesus of Nazareth rose from death, appeared to his disciples, and then "ascended to heaven." This alleged event, more than anything else, is traditionally regarded as warranting the claims mentioned earlier that Jesus in some sense embodied the authority and indeed the personal presence of the ultimate reality itself.

Part of what sets this claim apart is the fact that, more fully and dramatically than any other feature of Christian testimony, it seems vulnerable to every one of the sources of doubt we have considered so far. After all, if Christians are prepared to believe that something so spectacular happened to their founder, why withhold a similar assent from analogous claims about the founders of other religious traditions? And if the historical record of what occurred is problematic even in the case of Jesus' execution, which at least was an event reportedly witnessed by Jesus' enemies, what should one say about the fact that, according to the early Christians accounts themselves, Jesus' postmortem appearances were witnessed only by his followers? (The one apparent exception was Saul of Tarsus, who persecuted Christians until, on his own account, he was converted to their cause by his vision of the risen Jesus and assumed a new identity as the Apostle Paul. But by the time he testified to this event, Paul was hardly a disinterested observer!)

Again: if belief in miracles is rendered problematic by modern science, what miracle could be harder to accept than one involving the restoration to life and consciousness of a human body three days after its blood had ceased to circulate? Medical science knows all too well how rapidly cells not only cease to function but actually begin to dissolve; how quickly, for instance, a brain starved of oxygen permanently loses the capacity to sustain even the most minimal operations. Tissue damage throughout a cadaver is astonishingly rapid, and repairing it would require literally billions of miniscule interventions. And then there is the question of how something could remain in any meaningful sense a bodily entity and yet "ascend" into heaven, now that heaven can no longer be conceived, as it was in ancient times, as a space located somewhere above the solid dome of the sky.

Add to all those difficulties the kind of doubt inspired by the problem of evil—in this case, the problem of explaining why a benevolent deity would raise from the dead a single favored individual while leaving so many innocents in their graves. Is there any way to defend a claim so broadly besieged by all these reasons for doubt? And if there is not, what hope is there of winning a favorable hearing for the rest of what Christianity has to say about the significance of this particular human life?

Why not be agnostic?

We have now presented what we regard as the five most important reasons, at least at this particular moment in human history, for doubting that what the Christian traditions have to say about God and God's actions in the world—actions culminating (according to those traditions) in the events associated with the life, death, and resurrection of Jesus of Nazareth—is likely to be actually true. These are, first, the success of science in explaining formerly mysterious phenomena in strictly natural terms, without any need to invoke supernatural causes; second, the occurrence of terrible events that a God like the one Christians profess to believe in would presumably not permit; third, the existence of multiple religious traditions, each of which shares with Christianity a reasonable claim to success in fostering the moral virtue and spiritual growth of its adherents; fourth, the precarious state of the historical evidence on which Christian claims about Jesus are largely based; and fifth, the many different ways in which credulity is strained by the claim that Jesus rose from the dead.

These all seem to us powerful reasons for doubt, although our readers will certainly differ in their assessment of which are the stronger and weaker among them. One notes a marked tendency among Christian believers, and even among the theologians who act as spokespersons for the tradition, to turn away from these concerns, even castigating those who try to formulate them as enemies of the faith. But how is the Christian tradition to offer convincing arguments—arguments that can be taken seriously in the contemporary context—if its representatives do not seek to understand the predicament of belief in its full depth? More important still: how can it address the needs of those whose spiritual health it professes to nurture if it refuses to take seriously their reasons for doubting its claims?

Is one of the five objections more serious than the others? We have found that our own assessments tend to shift over time, depending on personal as well as public factors too numerous to consider. At times—say, after the Indian Ocean tsunami or an especially horrible massacre—the problem of evil may loom largest in one's awareness; at other, quieter times, the uncertain state of the historical evidence may seem the most troubling. Still, when one steps back from the heated battles between Christianity's critics and its present-day defenders, one recognizes that most of the disputes involve one or more of these five major objections.[12]

Faced with the seriousness of the objections, one wants to know: can—and, more important, *should*—the doubts they foster be overcome? Should a commitment to the viability of Christian claims be maintained in spite of them? In the rest of this book, we will lay out a case for a positive answer to that question. We will argue that it makes sense even for non-Christians to regard belief in at least some Christian claims—those that Christianity shares with other theistic religions—as rationally preferable to their rejection; that it is intellectually better, consequently, to affirm those claims than to deny them; better also than to refuse to affirm them. And we will also argue that it makes sense for those who find themselves engaging ultimate reality in and through their participation in the Christian tradition to have a similar attitude toward certain claims that are particular to that tradition and are not shared by others. Here again, we think it is better for those so situated to affirm the claims than to deny them. Better—but not beyond all shadow of doubt. Because we judge the reasons to affirm Christian claims, even for those who find themselves "inside" the tradition, to be only somewhat stronger than the reasons not to affirm them, we regard our position as a kind of *Christian minimalism*.[13]

Note that one can be a minimalist in two different senses: either by believing *fewer things* than many others in one's tradition, or by affirming that one's beliefs are only minimally more likely to be true than false. One minimalist might thus hold very orthodox beliefs but do so with a very high degree of uncertainty; another might hold her beliefs more strongly, but only because what she affirms is less controversial than what the Christian tradition has affirmed in the past. Different parts of the position we will be defending are minimalist in each of these two senses. And yet, as we hope to show, the arguments do not require one to be *maximally* minimalist—minimalist to the extreme— to the extent that some popular authors in the so-called historical Jesus debate (for example) have claimed.[14]

Indeed, there is a sense in which minimalism of that kind isn't really minimalist at all in our sense, because its proponents overestimate the strength of their reasons for supposing they know what *really* happened and use that supposed knowledge to "correct" the received testimony. They may be minimalists in what they believe, but they are maximalists in the confidence with which they believe it; for that reason, they are probably more accurately called liberals than minimalists. The kind of minimalist we have in mind, in contrast, holds Christian beliefs that are significantly constrained by philosophical objections and contemporary scientific consensus (which distinguishes her from more conservative evangelical or neo-orthodox believers) but also holds beliefs that, despite those constraints, she has reason to think do justice to the received testimony of the Christian tradition (which sets her apart from liberal believers in the sense just defined).

But surely, a reader will note, such a position must be a remarkably precarious one. New arguments and new ideas emerge all the time, and an argument that looks good today can look much worse tomorrow, even (or especially?) to the person who formulates that argument. What is to prevent minimalism from sliding into agnosticism, or out of commitment altogether? Why isn't a minimalist blown about by "every wind of doctrine"?

And, come to think of it, why isn't Christian minimalism just Christian agnosticism by another name? A minimalist thinks the reasons for affirming Christian claims are stronger than the reasons for denying them; but she may hold that the balance is only slightly in favor of the Christian claims. She is thus unable to say that she knows with certainty that these claims are true. What practical difference does it make whether one affirms something as only somewhat more probable than the alternatives, in contrast to simply not knowing *what* to believe? After all, it is perfectly possible that her reasons for affirming Christian claims, like her reasons for doubting them, will shift over time, so that those reasons will seem to her weaker or stronger, better or worse, in the future. And yet how can she not remain open to new evidence and new arguments that she encounters over the course of her life?

One could solve that problem by deciding to believe at some point in time and then paying no attention to evidence and arguments against one's belief in the future—the fideist option that we criticized earlier. Or one could solve it by resolving to be a Christian agnostic, that is, by remaining committed to Christian practices but concluding that there is just no way, even in principle, to tell whether Christian claims are likely to be true, or even plausible.

We doubt, however, that Christian agnosticism is really the sort of rational resting place that its advocates might claim it to be. Again, agnostics are those who claim that one *cannot* know whether the claims in question are true, and therefore that trying to find out is pointless— or at least irrelevant to the more urgent practical demands of human life.

We do agree with many commentators today that it is difficult to make the case for Christian belief—difficult, that is, to make a case that is, or even *should* be, convincing to those who do not already participate in the experience of Christian faith and practice. What separates us from Christian agnostics is, first, our unwillingness to decide in advance that no progress in assessing Christian claims can be made and, second, our conviction that pursuing the question of what is really the case, what is really true, is not just an intellectual game but an urgent *religious* responsibility. In fact, it is a responsibility precisely for those who find themselves, as we do, continually drawn to what it is least misleading, perhaps, to call simply "the gospel." Again, that conviction separates us just as much from the Christian *fideist*—the person who thinks we should just take everything "on faith"—as it does from the Christian agnostic. As different as they may be in other respects, the fideist and the agnostic are equally "dogmatic" to the extent that they are both closed to the possibility of ever making progress in finding out whether Christian claims may actually be true, and both unwilling to let the content of their beliefs be affected by new ideas or discoveries. Does this mean that agnosticism is always mistaken? Not at all. There may well be questions—historical, philosophical, and religious—that one has reason to think will never be answered. We happen to think, and it is the purpose of this book to show, that the most important questions raised by the claims of Christianity are not among those. But suppose they were. Suppose one decided that, in the last analysis, there was simply no way to tell—no good reason to say one way or the other—whether the universe was grounded in an ultimately benevolent reality, or whether Jesus and his followers were simply deluded. Where would that leave us?

In the long run, we think, it would not make sense to act in accordance with a set of claims one really saw no way at all of evaluating or confirming. As we suggested a moment ago, for a Christian to adopt such a religious "policy" (so to speak) would be inconsistent with the very religion she was trying to practice. For if that religion claims anything about the ultimate reality on which our existence depends, it claims that this reality has made something of itself known, and in such a way that human beings can respond to it. One does not need black-and-white decision procedures—"evidence that demands a verdict," as Josh McDowell once put it—in order to explore the various arguments for and against the core Christian claims and to assess their (evolving) adequacy.[15] One cannot know in advance that human inquirers will ever reach a final resolution. But one can be certain that, if we do *not* engage the reasons for doubt and belief, we will never know whether a reconciliation is possible.

That sounds good, the critic may reply; but if our reasons for affirming Christian claims really are only slightly better than our reasons for denying them, how can we achieve the level of commitment—the degree of fidelity or faith—that those claims also seem to require? Why aren't we contradicting ourselves just as much as the Christian agnostic?

Here one first glimpses what will be one of the most important claims made in this book. That claim is that the strength of one's practical commitment may and very often does exceed the certainty of one's belief. Against the agnostic we will be making the case that it is permissible actually to believe, even in cases where the "objective" evidence is very close to neutral. Of course, there is much to say about the nature of this belief, the claims one makes, and the subjective states associated with them. The fact that human believing outruns the more careful assessment process of the relevant communities of experts does not provide carte blanche to make just any claims to knowledge and truth. Nor is our position identical to that of the well-known Christian philosopher Alvin Plantinga, who describes core Christian beliefs as "properly basic" and thus as justified until they encounter a specific "defeater."[16] But, like Plantinga, we do reject one assumption that is common to many agnostics: that it is always wrong to form beliefs unless a case can be made that would convince a neutral observer.

It may not follow that commitment would make sense in the absence of *any* good reason to believe. But if we *do* have reason to believe—reason to believe, that is, that a claim of world-shattering, life-defining importance is more likely than not to be actually true—then we have reason not only to hope that this claim is actually true but to guide our thoughts and actions by that claim and its implications. Some readers may be disturbed to read in these pages that, in our judgment, certain traditional claims of Christianity do not quite meet this standard. Others may be surprised when we conclude, after carefully analyzing the reasons to doubt the traditional claims, that a case can still be made for affirming the most essential among them.

One limitation must be acknowledged from the outset: the case that we will make for Christian minimalism will have a different status for those whose beliefs have been shaped by the tradition and those whose beliefs have not. Some of our conclusions have, we think, a claim on the attention of all rational agents who are concerned about ultimacy. Others will be fully credible only to those whose experience of ultimacy has taken place within, and been interpreted by, the context of Christian belief and practice. Our hope is to be able to present at least some of these intra-Christian claims in such a way that those who stand outside the tradition will regard them as justified for people who have experienced ultimacy in these ways. In other words, we hope they will at least be able to make the counterfactual judgment: "*Had I had the experiences in question*, I would be justified in holding these beliefs."

Some other important Christian claims, if we are honest about the matter, will fail to meet this standard. In these cases we cannot expect non-Christians to say, "If a person has had such and such experiences, he is thereby justified in believing this claim to be true." In such cases, we will argue, Christians may still hold the beliefs in question. But they must acknowledge the very different nature of what and how they continue to believe. Belief—reasonable belief—is possible in the face of large doses of uncertainty, as long as one honestly acknowledges not only the evidence for the claim in question but also the reasons for doubting it. (We work through these distinctions in greater detail in Chapter 7.)

In short, a crucial result of our inquiry will be the realization that not all the claims we end up affirming will turn out to have the same degree of rational justification. As important as it is to test the rationality of one's beliefs, in the religious lives of most (if not all) believers there are some beliefs that go beyond what one can fully explain or justify, even to one's own satisfaction! Just as the strength of one's commitment can exceed the degree of certainty of one's beliefs, what one finds oneself believing can go beyond what one can defend in terms of publicly compelling reasons. Indeed, as one proceeds from general questions that cut across religious boundaries into the richer but far more specific territory of a particular tradition, it becomes more and more difficult to formulate the grounds for belief in ways that lend themselves to rational assessment.

That is one reason why this book cannot be read as a manual of Christian apologetics. We do not regard ourselves as offering "knock-down arguments" against, or for, the claims of Christian orthodoxy. Our aim is not to talk "all rational agents" into, or out of, belief in the most robust of Christian claims about the nature and significance of what occurred in the events surrounding the life of a certain ancient rabbi. We do indeed defend a way of understanding the natural world as stemming from a not-less-than-personal ultimate reality, a way of conceiving divine action that is compatible with scientific methods and results, and a way of interpreting the New Testament resurrection claims that we think remains plausible for men and women in the twenty-first century. But we pursue this project in full awareness of the depth of the predicament of belief in an era that is unusually (although not uniquely!) subject to reasons for doubt.

2

The ultimate reality

The fundamental question

C hristian claims, as we understand them, presuppose a certain hypothesis about what is ultimately the case. In the opening chapter, we stated that hypothesis as "the belief or wager that behind or beyond all things, at the beginning of everything we see and know, there exists an ultimate reality that in some sense intended us (or beings like us) to be here and—again in *some* sense—desires our flourishing." Because it is capable of something like intention and something like desire, this ultimate reality—call it the UR for short—must be conceived, on this hypothesis, as having properties at least similar to those of a person.

Also in Chapter 1, we listed what we take to be the most urgent of the many reasons for doubting whether this fundamental hypothesis about the UR is actually true. These include the extraordinary success of modern natural science in explaining much of what seemed to our ancestors to be mysteries so unfathomable that they demanded supernatural explanations; they also include the vast array of conflicting human religious and philosophical systems, many of which purport to explain the universe without appealing to our fundamental hypothesis. We considered the challenge posed by the undeniable reality of innocent suffering. It seems to many that a world in which such suffering occurs cannot be a world created or governed by anything like the just and benevolent "creator" that most versions of theistic belief—including most Christian versions—would seem to imply. (Since many consider this to be the greatest single challenge to the rationality of a Christian interpretation of human experience, we return to it in some detail in Chapter 3.) Finally, we considered reasons to doubt the historical veracity of the biblical texts, and in particular the central Christian claims about the life, death, and resurrection of Jesus of Nazareth—a complex and urgent challenge that will occupy us in Chapters 5 and 6.

Christian thinkers have adopted many strategies for confronting these reasons for doubting their most basic convictions, and the result is a literature rich in argument and anecdote. One could easily spend a lifetime sifting through the debates, to which many eloquent and thoughtful writers have contributed. As Christian minimalists, however, we come at the questions in a rather different way. Our approach is not to canvass all the possible responses that could be offered but to seek out the most plausible version of Christian theism that is still consistent with what we take to be the tradition's core commitments.

Others may feel that they can demonstrate the equal plausibility of more robust Christian theologies, those with much more extensive metaphysical commitments; we encourage them to present their positions and marshal the philosophical and scientific arguments in their defense. While we welcome their projects and wish them well, we write for a different audience—those who are uncertain that *any* form of distinctively Christian belief in God is still plausible in an age of science and religious pluralism. Such readers are put off by the complex concepts and foreign-sounding vocabulary of Patristic and medieval disputes. For them, the core question is much starker: is there *any* form of Christian belief at all that may still be plausible? If even a pared-down version of Christian theism fails to convince, there is little chance that the metaphysically more demanding accounts will fare better. By contrast, if this minimal account succeeds, perhaps systematic theologians can build upon and extend these results. At any rate, we write not for those who are already certain of all the details, but for those who wonder what, if anything, of the Christian tradition can stand up to close critical scrutiny. This essay in Christian minimalism, as we stated in the preface, is dedicated to them.

Why even *ask* about the ultimate?

To contemporary ears, all talk of the "ultimate reality" can sound suspiciously metaphysical. After all, despite some powerful rearguard action by certain antiscientific communities, we live in an age dominated by science and empirical methods for acquiring knowledge.

Haven't scientifically testable theories about the world now replaced metaphysical speculations of this sort, rendering them obsolete?

Metaphysical reflections are indeed suspect, in our view, when they compete head-to-head with scientific explanations of matters that lend themselves to scientific investigation. The reason is not that scientists never make mistakes. It is that science is the public practice of checking for errors and replacing inadequate theories with better ones. Commercial air travel is as safe as it is because, after each crash, authorities identify the cause and require changes to avoid a repeat. Science is the same sort of activity applied to beliefs about nature: theories are "built" and checked out against the world, and those that fare poorly are replaced by better ones. The results are not infallible, but conclusions that result from this feedback process are rationally preferable to conclusions derived from speculation alone.

Still, it's a mistake to think that science therefore becomes the authority for *all* questions. Even within "normal" science, new questions arise at the borders of each domain of inquiry.[1] The certainty we can have about the best-established results within chemistry does not extend to the disputes now taking place at the boundaries of theoretical physics, and even less to, say, speculations about "what preceded the Big Bang." When it comes to natural science as a whole, however far the reach of scientific knowledge is extended, there will always be questions that cannot be answered on scientific grounds alone. After all, for any set of natural laws, one can always ask, "Why these laws, rather than other laws?" Come to think of it, why should the universe be such that it is describable by laws at all? And finally, why should the universe be such that it is describable by the kinds of laws that human beings can identify and understand?

The last century brought about the greatest scientific progress ever achieved in such a short period. At the same time, its breakthroughs repeatedly raised new questions whose answers may well lie beyond the scope of the science that provoked them. Quantum physics, the science of the very small, is notorious for confronting us with philosophical questions that physics itself may never be able to answer—questions involving, for example, the indeterminacy of quantum reality, the role of observers or subjectivity in measurement (the problem of the "collapse of the wave function"), the reconciliation of quantum physics and general relativity, and the unification of all the forces of nature into a single, "grand unified theory" (GUT), perhaps at a level of reality forever inaccessible to experiment (as would be the case if string theory turned out to be true).

For these reasons, it is puzzling to watch scientists going on the lecture circuit to proclaim the death of all philosophical questions and their replacement by science alone. Probably the best-known example today is British biologist Richard Dawkins. Dawkins is (rightly) impressed by the progress in the biological sciences over the last 150 years. But that progress has led him to conclude that *nothing* now lies outside the scope of biological explanation—not even the fundamental assumptions of biology itself. The philosopher Daniel Dennett expresses a similar sentiment when he proclaims that Darwinism is the "universal acid" that will dissolve everything in its path.[2] Dawkins seems particularly confident that the empirical parts of biology suffice to demonstrate that all talk of God is a "delusion."[3] (In a *Time* cover story in November 2006 he put his point more carefully: "If there is a God, it's going to be a whole lot bigger and a whole lot more incomprehensible" than most people think—a conclusion that many religious believers would in fact endorse.) It doesn't take much reflection, however, to realize that precise empirical results are achievable only if the investigator makes certain assumptions about the nature of the reality being studied. Science itself cannot justify the most fundamental of those assumptions (e.g., the assumption that natural laws are unchanging) because science can't do anything at all without taking those assumptions for granted. In the history of Western thought such assumptions have generally been called metaphysical beliefs.

The success of natural science is not the only reason, however, that some reject altogether the idea of asking questions about the nature of the UR. Some theorists have argued that metaphysical questions have no cognitive content whatsoever; they are a kind of nonsense that only *seems* to make sense, like Edward Lear's description of the man from Dingle Bank who

> ... grew rabid-wroth, he did,
> If they neglected books,
> And dragged them to adjacent cliffs
> With beastly Button Hooks,
> And there with fatuous glee he threw
> Them down into the otion blue.[4]

According to the "verificationist principle," advanced by logical positivists in the middle of the last century, only "observation statements," and statements directly inferred from them, have genuine meaning; all other statements are, strictly speaking, meaningless. The highly influential philosophical school that advocated this principle suffered a complete collapse, however, in the decades that followed, when philosophers realized that the verificationist principle did not satisfy its own criteria for meaning: it was itself not based on, or derived from, any observation statement. So, if the principle was true, it must by its own lights be taken as meaningless!

Some interesting conclusions follow from the repeated failure of movements, such as logical positivism, that have sought to rule out metaphysical questions *tout court*. Human reason inevitably finds itself confronted with questions it cannot answer empirically. One cannot prove that these broader questions *are* answerable, of course. But nor can one prove that they are meaningless or inherently *un*answerable, since trying to do so entails resorting to the very kinds of arguments one is trying to place off limits.

What is the most rational way to proceed in the face of this situation? If one is unable, even in principle, to avoid engaging in some activity, it makes sense to engage in it as well as one can. One reason the authors of this book are minimalists is their conviction that all assertions about the UR are by their very nature provisional and somewhat tenuous. But if there is no way to avoid making at least some assumptions about the nature of UR—even if one's assumption is only that the UR is an unfathomable mystery—should we not attempt to reason as carefully as we can about those assumptions, testing them against the broadest feedback we can elicit and the most stringent objections we are aware of? If, despite our best efforts, we discover that there is no way to show that one assumption about ultimate reality is more plausible than another, we will have to draw the appropriate consequences. But how can we know until we've tried? That, at any rate, is the spirit with which we ask metaphysical questions in what follows.

The ultimacy of mind

We have just defended the reasonableness, indeed unavoidability, of asking metaphysical questions—questions, that is, about the nature of

the UR that underlies or "grounds" all that we know and experience—and at least attempting to answer them. Indeed, we have
suggested that any attempt to block the consideration of metaphysical
questions must itself take the form of a metaphysical argument; it
becomes the very thing it seeks to discourage. Of course one can
always refuse to take an interest in such questions, but one cannot
invalidate them on the basis of reasoned argument.

One of the questions that has preoccupied humanity across centuries
and cultures is whether UR is in any sense conscious or mindlike.
Many have affirmed that UR is personal, that is, that it shares certain
important qualities that we associate with ourselves as persons. But is
this claim still plausible? What reasons are there for thinking of UR as a
person, or indeed as anything *like* a person? Whatever grounds all things
is of course also the ground of us, who are personal beings. But this
does not automatically mean that it must itself be personal, any more
than the ground of colored things must be colored or the ground of
heavy things must be heavy. What exactly is it about finite beings who
are self-aware, self-transcending, conscious of but also awed and mys-
tified by death, and fascinated by ideas like goodness, truth, and
freedom—what is it about such beings that their very existence should
seem, at least to many of us, to demand an explanation that grounds
those properties in the ultimate source of existence itself?

After all, it isn't as if we don't have ways of explaining how a
particular species of finite persons—a species like *Homo sapiens*, for
instance—could have evolved on a planet like the one we inhabit.
Since Darwin's suggestion in *On the Origin of Species* in 1859 that the
process of natural selection could account for the gradual development
of more and more complex life forms, researchers have learned in
intricate detail about the processes of biological change and the evolution of complexity.[5] Biologists have detailed countless examples of the
emergence of new structures and functions, and in recent years micro-
biologists have been able to reconstruct the exact mechanisms by
which these evolutionary changes take place. Studies of the causal
interactions between biological and cultural evolution are shedding
new light on the evolution of human language and mentality, and
"evolutionary psychologists" are now using biology to explain human
behaviors that were once the exclusive domain of psychologists and
philosophers.[6] The combination of evolutionary theory, genetics,
systems biology, and ecology now seems able to parse even highly

complex phenomena such as human cultural and mental activity as expressions of the natural process of evolutionary emergence.

How, then, can the emergence of any phenomenon—including the emergence of persons—serve as evidence that the source of all reality must itself be (in some sense) personal? We no longer suppose, with the ancients, that like arises out of like, and therefore, for instance, that mind can only emerge out of mind.[7] Theories of evolutionary emergence offer an increasingly precise way of explaining how unlike arises out of unlike (life from nonlife, and mental properties from nonmental neuronal structures). Thus they would seem to defeat any simple effort to argue backwards from the emergence of persons to an ultimately personal source.[8]

Given the successes of the evolutionary sciences, then, one does not need a theory of the UR in order to explain scientifically how beings like us could have evolved in a universe initially characterized by physical forces only. This helps to clarify, once again, the difference between scientific and metaphysical explanation. Science, aided by theories of evolutionary emergence, can in principle explain the causal mechanisms by means of which physical and biological processes gave rise to life and eventually to beings like us. But it would seem that science cannot even in principle answer the larger question—the *metaphysical* question—of why the most fundamental processes should exist in the first place. One can dismiss this question as meaningless (a strategy mentioned earlier), but one cannot answer it by scientific means.

It is not at all inconsistent, consequently, for someone who accepts contemporary physics and biology to grant the power of these sciences to explain how particular phenomena arose from the processes of the natural universe and yet still maintain that the ultimate explanation of those phenomena lies outside the scope of those theories. Given the universe we have, the natural and social sciences can explain how phenomena like life and mind evolved within that universe. But they do not explain why a universe in which those phenomena are possible should exist in the first place.

In recent years, a number of scientists and philosophers have observed that the initial conditions of our universe—the precise physical laws and the values of fundamental physical constants such as the speed of light, the mass of the electron, and the Planck constant—had to be exactly what they were at the moment of the Big Bang in order for galaxies, stars, and eventually planets to take shape in a way that would make at least one planet capable of sustaining life. It is these physical regularities that made it possible for organisms to evolve and, eventually, to enjoy mental and even personal life. The conditions for life as we know it, it seems, are extremely special, depending sensitively upon the values of a large number of constants of nature. The empirical values of these constants might well have been different; had they been slightly so—in some cases by about 1 percent, and in some cases by as little as one part in a billion—life would have been impossible. Examples include the relative masses of the proton and neutron, the ratio of the number of particles to antiparticles, and the fine structure constant (the dimensionless strength of the electromagnetic force).

This recognition, which has come to be known as the "anthropic principle," has led many scientists to conclude that this universe is "fine-tuned" for life.[9] The fact that the initial state of the universe should supply exactly the required conditions for life, they argue, is so inherently improbable that it can't have been an accident; consequently, the universe must have been produced on purpose, by a being who intended that the universe be capable of (eventually) giving rise to beings like us.[10] One version of this argument that has gained a large public following, despite strong scientific evidence against its central claims and assumptions, is known as the argument from intelligent design.[11]

We will not explore the details of this heated controversy here, since a number of good books already address this topic.[12] Even if one is convinced that the most complex versions of the anthropic argument are rigorous enough to be judged as sound, they succeed not as scientific theories but as philosophical arguments. For that reason, it is unfortunate that so much ink has been spilled on the arguments that the intelligent design theorists advance to establish the "scientific" status of their claims, a fruitless debate that has distracted attention from the real issues. The crux of the matter lies at the level not of competing scientific theories but of deeper philosophical assumptions.

Here, it would seem, theists are on a stronger footing, since it does indeed appear that certain questions are left unanswered at the level of science-internal theories alone. For example, the very fact that the initial conditions of the universe were what they were, and therefore that there exists a universe in which intelligent life could evolve, seems to demand an explanation that goes beyond the processes of evolution itself. And the best available explanation, in the eyes of many who have reflected on this question, is that our universe was created, on purpose, with that possibility "in mind." If so, whatever the UR is, it must be capable of purposive action.

There is, however, a standard and oft-repeated skeptical response to this argument. Note that the argument proceeds from the conditions necessary for life to the conclusion that the UR must be capable of intentional action and therefore must be (something like) a person. Many physical cosmologists today answer that, for all we know, ours is only one of a great many of universes—perhaps an infinite number—each with its own initial conditions and its own natural laws. If that's the case, then it is not surprising that at least one of those universes would be such that it meets the conditions necessary to sustain the emergence of life and, eventually, of mind. Nor is it surprising that we would find ourselves in one of the universes that did happen to meet those conditions. After all, it is only in such a universe that beings like us *could* exist and therefore be in a position to wonder why their universe should support their existence.

In a slight variation on this objection to the anthropic arguments, a critic may deny that it makes sense even to ask whether the existence of persons in a given universe is surprising or not. That would amount (says this critic) to asking a counterfactual question about the universe as a whole: "Why is this a universe that includes persons rather excludes them?" or, in other words, "Why isn't this a different universe?" But we could only ask that question, the critic argues, if we were in a position to stand outside our universe and compare it with others. Critics who argue in this way are equally skeptical of the claim that we can know our universe to be an *improbable* one. They deny, in short, that it is even meaningful to attempt to make a rational choice between, on one hand, the view that the universe was designed to be this way and, on the other hand, the theory that our universe is only one member of a vast "multiverse."

The multiverse objections to theism deserve a serious hearing, even if there are reasons for asking whether the multiverse theory could ever be a testable scientific hypothesis, or for that matter even a coherent postulation.[13] But suppose one grants the reasonableness of thinking that our universe is only one of the countless universes that actually exist. Does that assumption really lay to rest the question of why there should exist a natural order capable of supporting the evolution of life and mind? Or does it merely shift the focus of that question from this particular universe to the total ensemble of universes—the multiverse itself—within which it was possible for life and mind to emerge?

For the sake of argument, let us imagine for a moment that there are indeed many different universes, and therefore many different sets of initial conditions and physical laws. That assumption might at first seem to show that there is no need to explain the existence of our particular universe, hence no need to explain why there exists at least one universe in which the evolution of intelligent life was possible. But it raises another explanatory question that will turn out to be just as difficult to answer unless one supposes that the UR is more than a collection of physical forces. All multiverse theories implicitly accept the possibility of making assertions that are true of the entire (presumably infinite) ensemble of existing universes. In particular, these theories require us to postulate that certain basic conditions hold across *all these universes*, for if there were no shared lawlike relations, no such theory would qualify as a scientific theory.[14]

Suppose, then, the multiverse theory is correct. Suppose, that is, that there is a set of trans-universal physical laws that make possible the existence of multiple universes. We must ask, in that case, what it means that all universes have something in common, namely, that all are dependent on shared principles of order that we call, metaphorically, physical "laws." What would this fact (if it is a fact) say about the underlying UR that is implied by the existence of the multiverse itself?

Clearly such laws would transcend the physical conditions of every particular universe that exists within the ensemble of universes as a whole. But physical events as we know them only occur in *particular* universes. After all, our notion of what physical events are depends entirely on our observations of one particular universe—namely, the one we live in! So whatever they are, the laws that hold across all the universes in the multiverse cannot themselves depend on or be derived from any single universe. If these laws do not depend on any physical universe, could they have preceded all universes? In principle, yes, but not as descriptions of physical regularities. Before any universe existed, the laws of multiverse physics—the laws that multiverse theory needs if it is to be physics—were not yet "instantiated." There was as yet nothing that existed to instantiate them; they were pure potentials, pure possibilities. They were not physical things but the principles by which physical things belonging to each of the many universes would be "governed." But if they were not physical things, what kind of thing were they? And in what did they "reside" if not in a physical universe?

If we ask what kinds of thing in our experience, besides physical laws, can be instantiated by physical things but can also be described independently of the particular things that instantiate them, the obvious answer is *mental* things: ideas, images, concepts, thoughts. I can think of a tree without there existing a particular tree of which I am thinking; I can think of a unicorn without there existing any unicorn at all. To say that the laws of physics hold apart from the existence of any particular physical universe is to say that physical laws are more like concepts than they are like physical things. And where might (something like) a concept reside if not in (something like) a mind?[15]

These reflections show that someone who wants to characterize the UR in strictly physical terms faces a serious dilemma. If she accepts the notion that there is only one universe, she is confronted by striking evidence of fine-tuning that at least seems to suggest that our universe was intentionally framed with initial conditions that would be conducive (in the long run) to the emergence of intelligent life. If, on the other hand, she rejects the fine-tuning argument and affirms the theory that ours is only one of innumerable universes, she then finds herself subscribing to a framework of universe-transcending laws, which in turn implies the existence of a mindlike realm that precedes or transcends the infinite succession of physical universes. Either way, she ends up with an interpretation of the UR that conceives it as mindlike. In one case, the UR might be an intentional agent who purposely created the only universe that exists; in the other case, it might be a mindlike realm of principles or laws on which the many universes within the multiverse depend for their very existence.

From mind to agency

In the foregoing sections, we have laid out a case for the view that everything we know and experience has its ultimate source in a reality that is more like mind than matter. Even if there are multiple universes in addition to the only one we can observe, we have reason to suppose that there is a set of ordering principles or laws that underlies them all, and we have reason to suppose that those laws must have their source in (something like) a mind.

That conclusion, however, is only part of the hypothesis we set out to defend at the beginning of this chapter. The full hypothesis was not just that the UR had (something like) mental properties. It included the idea that the UR was not just a kind of mind but also a kind of *agent*, capable of forming something akin to what we call intentions and acting in accordance with them. In particular, the hypothesis included the notion that the UR was such that it was capable of having beings like us (benevolently) in mind; that it desired their existence and, indeed, their flourishing, and acted to bring about the existence of at least one universe in which it would be possible for them to exist and to flourish. Only in that case, after all, would it make sense for us to regard the UR as a personal (or, at least, *not less than personal*) being with whom we might interact in the ways suggested in the previous chapter. And only if *that* makes sense will it be plausible to suppose that the UR may have become involved in human history in anything like the way suggested by the most important claims of Christian theism, no matter how minimalistically those claims are to be understood.

Why should we suppose, then, that the UR is more than mind*like* and is, in fact, a kind of agent—that is, a mind that is capable of performing purposeful actions, which it must be if we are to regard the creation of the universe (or multiverse) in anything like Christian terms? This question is fairly easy to answer if we accept the claim that there is only one physical universe: the fine-tuning evident in the initial conditions of our universe (if it's the only one), when combined with the mindlike nature of UR, strongly suggests that this universe was endowed on purpose with conditions ultimately conducive to the emergence of intelligent life. (Again, note that this is a philosophical argument and not, as the "intelligent design" theorists have claimed, an argument claiming the status of a scientific theory.) But even if one accepts the multiverse theory—which was designed, at least in part, precisely to avoid the implications of fine-tuning—it remains more plausible to affirm than to deny the reality of a mindlike source of the regularities that hold across the vast array of universes and that (according to multiverse advocates) explain the relationships among them.

Suppose the UR is mindlike but also that there are, or may be, multiple universes. What then? Perhaps the multiverse arises from the UR by a kind of necessity; perhaps the mindlike reality that is the source of all that exists is simply such that it necessarily (automatically, involuntarily) produces that which is other than itself. An interesting speculation, but what reason do we have, or *could* we have, to think that this speculation was actually true?

Perhaps, however, the multiverse just happens to "emanate" from its mindlike source, not by necessity but by some process or mechanism of which we have and *can* have no idea. Again, that is an intriguing notion; indeed, it's one with a substantial pedigree in the history of Platonic and Neo-Platonic thought.[16] But to accept it would be to leave the relation between the physical universe and its mindlike source entirely unexplained. It would leave us with two distinct realities, of two radically different kinds—the physical universe and the mindlike UR; it would tell us that these very different kinds of reality must have something to do with each other; but it would offer us no prospect of ever understanding what that "something" might be. We noted earlier that settling for a metaphysical dead end of that kind was always a possible outcome of asking ultimate questions. What remains unclear is why it would ever count as rational to accept such a final theory as long as we had another option.

And there *is* another option: namely, to understand the emergence of the universe or multiverse from its mindlike source on the model of the production of a physical effect by a mental cause—or in short, on the model of an intentional action. Unlike the first two options, this one does provide us with an explanation of the relation between the mindlike UR and the multiverse: that the former reality is a kind of agent, and that this agent intentionally brought about the existence of the latter reality.

With that step, we arrive at the conclusion that the universe we see around us—or the multiverse to which that universe belongs—is best understood as the product of a mindlike and agentlike UR that purposely brought about its existence. We believe that this is the most justified position, the one that can best stand up to objections by those who are experts both in the relevant sciences and in the metaphysical debates concerning these topics.

What are those objections? They tend to fall into two broad categories. Those in the first category charge that one cannot speak of the UR as mind or mindlike without falling into an illicit projection of human experience and categories onto the ultimate. David Hume's classic criticisms of arguments for the existence of God, and especially of the teleological proof, are usually cited in support of this claim.[17] But the minimalist argument we have developed here does not seek to maximize parallels between humans and God; it draws back even from the standard claim that "God is a person." To acknowledge that the overall data are best explained by an account of reality that includes minds and the mental predicates they apprehend[18] does not open the door to any simple projection of human traits onto the divine. The argument given above turns instead on the possibility of a successful scientific cosmology—a very different form of reflection than the teleological proof.

A second set of objections maintains that it is impossible in principle to decide between personal and impersonal understandings of the UR. Because some religions (and philosophies) attribute personal or mental properties to the UR whereas others affirm a UR that transcends all such attributes, it is argued, the best solution is to conceive the UR as beyond the personal–impersonal distinction altogether. Note, however, that this response, famously advanced by John Hick,[19] shares some of the weaknesses of the "permanent agnostic" view that we discussed in Chapter 1. Rather than evaluating new arguments for mindlike versus nonmindlike conceptions of the UR, it attempts to stand above the fray and proclaim all views equally true (and hence equally false).

This metaphysical theory—namely, that "the Real" exists beyond the personal–impersonal distinction altogether—is sometimes put forward in the name of the so-called Eastern religious traditions. In fact, however, conceptions of the UR as fundamentally mindlike are much more widespread across the world's religious traditions than proponents of this view admit. Take, for example, the Hindu philosopher Sankara, who is often cited as a pure pantheist because he speaks of the UR as "Brahman without attributes" (*nirguna Brahman*). Yet Sankara still affirms consciousness and bliss as two of the three primary qualities of the Ultimate—distinctively mindlike traits.

Note also that attributing mindlike or personlike qualities to the UR does not require one to deny that it has any other types of qualities. In fact, philosophers have shown a number of ways in which impersonal qualities might exist alongside mindlike aspects. Although the discussions are rather technical, it is not hard to see how both kinds of qualities, rather than cancelling each other out, actually play complementary roles when one attempts to speak of the UR. Examples include the distinction between the "primordial ground" and the emerging personal aspects of God drawn by the nineteenth-century Idealist philosopher Schelling, later echoed by the theologian Paul Tillich, and the distinction between the primordial and consequent "poles" of God in the work of the process philosopher Alfred North Whitehead.[20] Similar examples can be found across the religious and philosophical traditions, providing further ways to model this understanding of the UR.[21]

We first showed that it was difficult to demonstrate the impossibility of metaphysics without falling into self-contradiction (doing the very thing one is trying to dismiss) and then moved on to argue that the most adequate conception of the UR was one that ascribed to it mindlike qualities. But it's important to note what, so far, we have *not* shown. The notion of agency we have so far applied to the UR is an extremely limited one; it's a notion of agency that falls far short of what people usually have in mind when they refer to the UR as "God." We have not yet said anything that would suggest that the UR is the *summum bonum* (the "highest good"); that the UR has benevolent intentions toward beings outside itself, let alone that it is "omnibenevolent"; or that the UR exercises a "providential" care for the world or its inhabitants. Indeed, we haven't shown that the UR has any moral or ethical qualities whatsoever. We still need to ask whether what matters to the UR has anything to do with what matters to us. Unless we can provide a plausible answer to that question, the hard metaphysical work we have done in this chapter so far will prove to be of little value to theists in general, or to Christians in particular.

Creation and the love of others

Suppose we have succeeded in showing that it makes more sense to regard the ultimate source of all that exists as a kind of mind than as a collection of mindless forces and events. This mindlike reality must be inconceivably more powerful than any we encounter in our mundane experience; it isn't just one mind among many but the source of all other minds, and indeed of the universe—or perhaps all the many universes—in which those other minds have come into existence. We have also provided a reason for supposing that this mind is not just an impersonal cause of what exists but a kind of intentional agent who created the universe (or universes) on purpose. But even if we stipulate that the UR is both a mind and a purposeful agent, we still have to ask why one should take the further and—for our overall hypothesis—crucial step of supposing that the UR has any interest in the things that interest *us*, or in any way cares about the things *we* care about.

At least since Hume's *Dialogues Concerning Natural Religion* (1779), philosophers have been keenly aware of how difficult it is to argue for the goodness of God from the natural world as we find it. Given a universe that is as morally ambiguous as the one we inhabit, it has seemed manifestly implausible to claim that we inhabit the "best of all possible worlds," as Leibniz notoriously put it. We therefore propose to approach the question differently. We begin by asking what conclusions about the moral nature of the UR follow from the assumption that the UR has intentionally brought about the existence of a universe in which it was possible for rational and moral agents—that is, for persons—to evolve.

In the next chapter, we will show why an interest in producing a universe that would support the development of finite persons requires the UR to impose certain constraints on the exercise of its own power. The resulting picture of the UR's creative action has some affinities with what theologians call *kenosis*, a Greek term that means "an emptying" and whose theological application derives from an early Christian hymn, quoted by Paul in one of his letters, about the self-abnegation or humility of Jesus the Christ (Philippians 2:7). What Jesus reportedly did in voluntarily subjecting himself to suffering and death has become a model, according to the newer "kenotic" tradition in theology, for understanding the self-limitation by which God brought into existence a world outside the divine reality itself.[22] What does such self-limiting action tell us, however, about the UR's nature, or its relation to human values?

One cannot assume, after all, that the mere fact of an agent's taking an interest in the existence of other beings is morally admirable, even if it entails a certain amount of self-limitation on that agent's part. One thinks of numerous mundane analogs: the farmer who shows concern for the well-being of his livestock only for the sake of maximizing his own financial gain; the would-be father who works long hours so he can start a family but who mainly wants children out of loneliness or for any of a host of social or cultural reasons; the teacher who pours her life into the minds of her students because she sees them as a way of establishing her career and exerting influence over the future of her profession. The motives involved in each of these cases are not obviously evil and do not involve any sort of deception; but neither are they altruistic.

An obvious reply is that we are not aware of any ulterior motive on the UR's part, and therefore we should assume that the UR created a universe in which we would exist simply for our sake—that is, out of *love* for us—and not in the service of some other purpose. But consider a perfectly plausible ulterior motive for the UR to bring about the existence of sentient beings other than itself: in order to expand its own experience to include theirs. Why not suppose that the UR created the universe (or multiverse) only with the goal of introducing genuine novelty into its own experience, say out of a sort of cosmic boredom? Perhaps that is the only reason the UR wanted to create finite agents with enough autonomy that they would not simply be projections of its own will. In short, there seems to be at least one plausible reason, other than love of others, for a divine being to want to limit its power in order to bring about the existence of creatures like us.[23]

But is such an ulterior motive really plausible when ascribed to what we have every reason to regard (prior to its own self-limitation) as a being of *infinite* power? Note that in each of the mundane examples mentioned above, the ulterior motives in question were expressions of a certain insufficiency, a certain lack on the part of the human agent who performed the (strategically) self-limiting action. It might at first seem plausible to suppose that an infinite being could have a similar ulterior motive. If that were true, the UR would be limiting itself only in a *strategic* way, as a human being might, when it withheld its power in order to allow the emergence and development of finite rational agents like us.

But when one actually tries to imagine what ulterior motive a UR might have for doing such a thing, each of the possibilities turns out to be incoherent. They all imply some sort of insufficiency, some lack of power or knowledge; but none of these limitations makes sense when imagined as a motive for a mind that constitutes the ultimate reality.

Why, after all, would an infinite being need or want to share in the experience of other beings in order to complete itself? If this being is truly infinite, contemplation of itself will presumably provide all the richness and novelty that contemplating the experience of other beings could ever provide. (In fact, precisely this was Aristotle's conception of

God or what he called *nous noetikos*, "thought thinking itself.") If it creates beings other than itself, the infinite being must be doing so not for its own sake—it doesn't *need* those others—but for the sake of those others themselves.

Again, *we* need others. In fact, the contemplation of our finite selves, in isolation from any broader communal or spiritual context, quickly becomes a source of nausea or claustrophobia, leading to despair or madness. But for an infinite being, the contemplation of itself is already the contemplation of an infinite richness.[24] So if it chooses to bring about the existence of beings other than itself—which necessarily means, if it chooses to bring about the existence of finite beings— the infinite being must be doing so out of what, resorting to admittedly anthropomorphic terms, we can only regard as sheer generosity: sheer love for the finite others for whose sake it chooses to limit its own infinite power.

Earlier we introduced the theological term *kenosis*, for the self-limiting mode of action the UR must undertake in order to permit the development of beings other than, and independent of, itself. We can now add another Greek term, *agape*, naming a kind of love: specifically, the kind of selfless love that, in contrast to the kind denoted by the term *eros*, focuses on the well-being of the loved one rather than on the needs of the self.[25] Once again, we have been led to ascribe this disposition to the UR by reflecting on the reason an infinite being might wish to bring about the existence of beings other than itself.[26]

The divine lure

Our reflections on the UR's intentions have been restricted so far to what can be inferred from the sheer fact of creation. But there is another, very different source of insight that, in our view, sheds significant light on this question.

What we have in mind is closely related to the intriguing exploration by the sociologist Peter Berger of what he has called "signals of transcendence,"[27] that is, human experiences that seem to point in the direction of an ultimate and ultimately benevolent reality, even if they fall short of counting as sufficient evidence that such a reality actually obtains. Perhaps the most important such signal, for present purposes, is the experience of being guided by what is traditionally known as *conscience*. In the next chapter we will present an argument for keeping open the possibility that the UR may be involved in interactions with finite persons and that the content of such interactions may involve the UR's providing human beings with moral guidance.

Of course, showing that divine communication through human conscience is a theoretical possibility does not yet give us reason to think that such communication has actually occurred in any given case. In fact, without some reason for supposing that the UR is an agent whose values include ideals toward which it makes sense for human beings to aspire, it is hard to see why one would ever be justified in regarding an experience of inner moral admonition or discovery—the "voice of conscience"—as involving actual input from the UR, rather than as a strictly natural phenomenon involving the interaction of individual minds with whatever social norms they may have internalized.

But the arguments in the preceding section gave us at least one reason for supposing that the UR is an agent who cares about at least some of what we care about. If the grounds for creation were not necessity or need but selfless love or *agape*, it is unclear what grounds one has to deny that human experiences of moral illumination might sometimes be shaped, inspired, or guided by the "lure" of the ultimate reality. Indeed, it is unclear on what grounds one would deny that the guidance of the UR might play a significant role in the development of (individual and corporate) human values and in human reflection on the best way to pursue them. At a minimum, that hypothesis is consonant with the outcome of the metaphysical arguments presented in the earlier sections of this chapter.

Although it falls short of evidential confirmation in any strict sense, such coherence supports the plausibility of the broadly theistic hypothesis that the UR is an agent capable of reaching out to other agents in acts of intentional communication—acts that, if they are to operate through what we call the "voice of conscience," must be at least as rich in content as our highest values are. An agent that we have reason to think addresses us in this way is certainly an agent we have reason to regard as more like a person than an impersonal force.

If the UR is indeed a personal (or, as we would prefer to say, a not *less* than personal) agent, and if that agent is indeed motivated by the kinds of values and intentions (or something like values and intentions) that we have been describing, then we are not very far removed at this point from the vision of ultimate reality embodied in the Abrahamic traditions. Those traditions all yield, after all, a vision of the UR as an infinite agent who is not less than personal and who has performed at least one self-limiting act of creation motivated by *agape*, that is, by a love of others from whom one needs nothing in return.

Those who have followed the foregoing exposition carefully will realize, however, that one cannot actually *derive* the notion of God in the Abrahamic traditions from the arguments given in this chapter. Arguments for a mindlike or agentlike understanding of the UR are not the same as apologetic arguments that aim to show the existence and activity of the God of Abraham, Isaac, and Jacob or, for that matter, the God and Father of Jesus Christ. There is a significant gap between these two kinds of projects—the same gap to which we drew attention in the previous chapter. Rather than obscuring that gap, we again draw attention to it here, as we will continue to wrestle with it in the chapters to come. As much as one might wish it to be different, many of the values that we identify most closely with the God portrayed by the Christian tradition simply cannot be established or defended at the level of general argumentation—the level on which we have been operating—independent of particular strands of religious experience and testimony. (We return to this theme at the beginning of Chapter 5.)

Nevertheless, it is impossible not to notice how close the concept of the UR at which we have arrived stands to what the theistic traditions have meant by the notion of God. Theists conceive ultimate reality as an infinite personal reality, a reality that has no intrinsic need of the others whom it freely and lovingly creates.[28] We seem then to have arrived at, or close to, a theistic view of UR. Indeed, this theism or almost-theism might also be said to have a "christological tinge," insofar as it conceives the UR as intrinsically involving the compassionate and self-giving relation to others that is associated, in Christian thought, with the character and actions of a particular human being.

For reasons that will become clearer in Chapter 4, this last connection cannot be construed as a theistic proof, a demonstration of the existence of (say) the Christian God from universal principles of reason or morality that are (supposedly) evident to all rational agents. Nevertheless, the *concept* of the UR that has emerged from this and the previous chapter is close enough to the concept of God in Abrahamic theism that, from this point on, we will frequently use the term "God" to describe the vision of the UR that we are exploring. As soon as we do this, however, we are confronted with what may be the weightiest reason to reject belief in the existence of a God who cares—or indeed is capable of caring—about the values of finite creatures.

3

Divine action and the argument from neglect

The argument from neglect

Not everyone thinks the universe is grounded in an ultimate reality (UR) of the kind we have been describing. Even among those who accept the existence of a divine reality, not everyone agrees that this reality is (something like) a person, insofar as personhood is understood as entailing rational agency, that is, the capacity and disposition to perform intentional actions that bring about particular states of affairs.

More than any other single factor, we believe, what accounts for the reluctance even of some convinced theists to embrace a personalistic picture of the ultimate reality is the perception that the acts we would expect a divine agent to perform do not occur. Above all, the acts we would expect to occur but that seem not to are acts that would prevent or relieve the egregious cases of innocent suffering that we observe all around us. These are acts that we would expect a *benevolent* divine agent to perform; their nonoccurrence raises the possibility that the UR is a malevolent person, or perhaps an amoral one. But, for most versions of personalistic theism, an evil or amoral divine reality would be even worse news than an impersonal one.

The inference from the apparent nonoccurrence of expected divine actions to the rejection of personalistic theism has been usefully dubbed "the argument from neglect" by one prominent nonpersonalistic theist, Wesley Wildman. Here is a passage in which he eloquently summarizes that argument:

Of course, it is not actually the existence of suffering that is the problem for personal ideas of God. That is a shared challenge for all religions and all theologies. It is what a supposedly personal active God doesn't do about it that is the problem. Consider the following analogy. When my children endanger themselves through their ignorance or willfulness, I do not hesitate as one trying to be a good father to intervene, to protect them from themselves, to teach them what they don't know, and thereby to help them become responsible people. I needed to do that a lot more when they were little than I do now but I believe that my love for those children can be measured as much by my interventions as by my allowing them space to experience making their own decisions independently. They do need to experience the effects of their choices, whether good or bad, but I would rightly be held negligent as a parent if I allowed them such freedom that they hurt themselves or others out of ignorance or misplaced curiosity or wickedness.

To the extent that we think of God as a personal active being, we inevitably apply these standards. Frankly, and I say this with the utmost reverence, the personal God does not pass the test of parental moral responsibility. If God really is personal in this way, then we must conclude that God has a morally abysmal record of inaction or ineffective action. This I shall call the *argument from neglect*, and I take it to be the strongest moral argument against most forms of personal theism. It applies most obviously to versions of personal theism in which God is omnipotent. But the argument from neglect also applies to views of personal theism that deny omnipotence, such as process theology, because the argument establishes that God's ability to influence the world is so sorely limited as to make God virtually irrelevant when it comes to the practical moral struggles of our deeply unjust world.[1]

To meet this objection, a defender of personalistic theism has to do two things: first, show that there may be a good reason why a personal and active God, if there is one, either cannot or chooses not to perform the acts we would expect a benevolent God to perform; second, avoid what is in effect the *reductio ad absurdum* of constraining divine action so extensively that it becomes pointless or irrelevant. This chapter is devoted to addressing these two challenges.

Now the set of possible divine motives is presumably infinite, and the set of possible constraints on divine action may also be infinite. We do not think it is sufficient, for that reason, merely to show the logical possibility that there is a good reason for what looks like divine neglect.[2] Nor, at the opposite extreme, would we be so bold as to claim to *know* what reason God actually has, or even to claim that we can establish this with, say, a probability of greater than 0.5. Instead, we would like to know whether there is an account of divine motives and divine action that would constitute a *plausible* explanation for apparent divine neglect—plausible, that is, in the eyes of the relevant community of inquiry, which in this case means a community not already closed to the possibility of personalistic theism. Ideally, such an explanation would be sufficiently plausible that, at least in the long run, the community would come to regard it as superior to its competitors. But as long as it gives a plausible and consistent explanation of why a benevolent God would refrain from intervening in cases where we would otherwise expect such a being to do so, it will count, in our view, as successfully defeating Wildman's objection to the claim that the UR is more aptly conceived in personal than in nonpersonal terms.

Responses to the argument from neglect

With that aim in mind, it seems to us that the best place to begin is with a hypothesis general enough to embrace the many phenomena that might be mentioned in support of the argument from neglect but concrete enough to embody those assumptions about the nature and intentions of God that have emerged from the theistic traditions. As it turns out, defending this hypothesis requires one not only to reflect on innocent suffering but also to appeal to conclusions in a number of other fields, including scientific knowledge about the natural world, fundamental considerations in the philosophy of science and the philosophy of mind, and the role of kenotic thinking in recent christologies. Although in the present chapter we cannot develop the full formal argument across all these fields, we do indicate the range of topics that must be addressed by parties on both sides of the debate. Here, then, is the hypothesis with which we propose to answer the argument from neglect:

Suppose the purpose, or at least one purpose, of God's creating our universe was to bring about the existence of finite rational agents capable of entering into communion with God.[3] Suppose the way God achieved that purpose was by creating a universe in which events would be consistently governed by regularities of the kind described by the laws of physics or, more broadly, the laws of nature. Because the universe operates according to its own internal regularities, beings who evolve through the operation of those regularities are not simply the direct expressions of the divine will (as would be the case if they were directly created by divine fiat) but partake of the (relative) autonomy with which God has endowed the universe as a whole.[4]

Everything else that we have to say about the argument from neglect follows from this fundamental hypothesis, which of course will require elaboration before its relevance to that argument can fully emerge. But questions about it immediately arise. Perhaps the most important are these: First, how regular do the regularities have to be? Why can't God preserve the regularities just enough to bring about the evolution of rational and autonomous beings but suspend their operation whenever necessary to prevent innocent suffering? Second, if God *can't* suspend the regularities of nature, why suppose that God can perform any actions at all within the created universe?

First response

The first of these questions turns out to be the easier one to answer, because the answer follows rather quickly from an analysis of the conditions under which autonomous agents can evolve. The second is more challenging, because it requires us to identify at least one sphere of activity in which divine acts would not constitute suspensions of natural laws and then to show why God's ability to act in that sphere does not raise, all over again, the specter of either divine inconsistency or divine neglect.

Turning, then, to the first question: why can't God suspend the regularities of nature whenever God has reason to do so? Consider a universe in which God could and did suspend at will the operation of (to begin with) physical regularities, a world (say) in which the murderer's bullet turned into a flower when it left his gun and floated gently to the ground. Could rational and autonomous beings—beings, that is, at least as rational and autonomous as we human beings appear to be—evolve in such a universe? Perhaps they could reach our level of biological complexity, as long as God preserved enough physical regularity to sustain the right mechanisms of mutation and selection. But could they function in the universe with the kind of self-determination or autonomy we seem to have?

It is hard to see how the evolution of rational agency, not to speak of moral agency, would be possible in such a world. Could beings in such a world, for instance, come up with natural science in anything like the form we know it?

It seems that they could not, because they would have no basis for developing, or at least developing fully, the appreciation of natural regularities on which science depends. Imagine that scientists became convinced that God regularly changed the outcomes of physical events in a counterfactual and nonlawlike manner, and imagine (for the sake of argument) that they were right. That is, imagine they knew that God regularly set aside natural regularities and intervened in the natural world according to hidden divine purposes and that, were God *not* to act in this manner, the phenomena that they observed would not have occurred. Even if the scientists could never in fact catch God red-handed, as it were (because no observation or experiment could actually detect these exceptions to natural law), it seems clear that they could not pursue the expansion of knowledge in the natural sciences in the way we now do. For one would always be unsure whether some natural pattern was really lawlike, or merely an artifact of God's happening to intervene in similar ways over a particular span of time. Moreover, one would never know when the actual laws of nature might suddenly be set aside for the sake of some overriding divine purpose. The self-understanding of science would be radically changed, and indeed its motivation would be radically diminished.

Why should it matter, however, whether science as we know it is possible? After all, the institution of science is, in one sense, the contingent product of a certain strand of human social and cultural history. In another sense, however, science as we know it is a systematic mechanism for managing a far broader and arguably inescapable process: namely, the fixation of human belief through the shared investigation of a universe that is sufficiently stable to permit such investigation.[5] In that sense, science is merely one institutional expression of the more general human project of individual and collective self-definition and self-determination, which proceeds by our interacting with a reality that we can come to understand, in no small measure because it is *not* subject to arbitrary alteration by human—or more than human—fiat. (Intentional alterations by human agents who have evolved within the world and remain dependent on its physical conditions are not, of course, excluded by this principle.)

In short, we assume that the rationality and autonomy of finite individuals both depend upon and entail participation in what C. S. Peirce would have called a "community of inquiry."[6] A community of inquiry can foster and express the development of rationality only if it proceeds on the assumption that whatever it investigates is, at least in principle, capable of being investigated, that is, progressively examined and re-examined by successive members of the community in question. In this case, what is true of the community is also true of individuals: we can only develop a sense of (relatively) autonomous selfhood if the objects around us have reasonably stable properties.

Suppose we stipulate, then, that both individuals and communities of inquiry can only develop if they assume that the world around them is safe from arbitrary alteration on a regular basis by supernatural forces. Let's call this the *regularity argument*. This argument still leaves unclear why a sufficiently powerful divine agent could not at least *occasionally* intervene to override physical regularities. One can perhaps see that if God always intervened to prevent innocent suffering of any magnitude whatsoever, these frequent abrogations of natural law would sooner or later deprive us of the ability to perceive ourselves as persons separate from others, or indeed as beings separate from God. But why should God refrain from intervening on at least some of those occasions where a brief suspension of natural regularities would prevent a tremendous evil? For instance, God might not act to prevent my every injury and yet still might act to prevent the kind of brief and local seismic event that triggered the Indian Ocean tsunami in December 2004, which in a matter of a few hours took more than a quarter million lives and inflicted unimaginable suffering on the even larger number of survivors. Or why could God not have surreptitiously caused Hitler to die in his sleep before he was able to carry out, among other evils, the systematic extermination of European Jews?[7]

The question is a reasonable one, and in fact it goes right to the heart of the argument from neglect. The answer, we suggest, is that creating and sustaining a universe in which free rational agents can evolve and act turns out, upon reflection, to be an either–or affair. A benevolent God could not intervene *even once* without incurring the responsibility to intervene in every case where doing so would prevent an instance of innocent suffering. Call it the *not-even-once* principle.

Why, however, should that be the case? What kind of necessity is it that would compel a benevolent God to act with such consistency? Is the necessity a *forensic* one (because God would have no way of explaining to others why God had not also intervened in other cases)? Would it in fact be *unethical*, because unfair, for God to intervene only in certain cases but not all? Or is the God–universe relation *metaphysically* such that the universe can only remain autonomous if God never acts upon it coercively, perhaps because a single act of divine coercion would somehow (perhaps through some kind of chain reaction?) automatically subject the universe as a whole to the direct and therefore absolute control of the divine will?

The forensic option seems too anthropocentric; why should God worry about being criticized by the likes of us? The ethical explanation is better but, as initially stated, perhaps not fully convincing; why couldn't God remove any unfairness by adjusting the degree of divine intervention according to such criteria as the severity of the suffering, or the amount of disruption needed to prevent or stop it—much as we humans do when establishing our own policies for intervention in cases ranging from child protection to disaster relief to full-scale regime change? The fact that we often decide badly does not permit us to eschew intervention altogether; still less, one might argue, should God be let off the moral hook. (We will return to this issue of what might be called "proportional intervention" in a moment.)

The third option is perhaps the most intriguing to those of a metaphysical bent, but it poses the conceptual as well as theological risk of positing a quasi-Gnostic gulf between God and God's creation. Why, for instance, would a benevolent God create a universe with which that God had no intention of interacting? This option has the further disadvantage of invoking a rather fanciful causal mechanism—the metaphysical "chain reaction"—of which we have no actual concept or evidence.

It is not obvious that the forensic, ethical, and metaphysical responses are fatally flawed; each one may offer some support for the "not even once" principle. But given the sorts of reservations that one might raise against the three explanations just canvassed, it behooves the theist to look for a more rigorous response. We believe that a combination of the ethical and metaphysical responses provides a more compelling defense of the not-even-once principle than either by itself. Suppose we begin by looking more closely at the reason we mentioned for resisting the ethical defense of the principle. The critic wonders why God can't do what human agents at least *try* to do. We humans proportion the scale and frequency of our interventions to the magnitude of the harms they are intended to stop or prevent and to the risk of greater harm they pose. Does it make sense to impose on God a similar responsibility to intervene when the conditions are right for doing so?

Here is a reason to think that this does *not* make sense. From a human point of view, it is relatively easy to identify what we regard as cases of actual or potential suffering that are so great that we consider ourselves bound to intervene to stop or prevent them. But, as is often pointed out in a case like the international response to the Asian tsunami, our ability to make such discriminations is powerfully dependent on the limitations both of our attention and our resources. We quickly suffer from "compassion fatigue," which is all the more reason why we not only can but must be discriminating in choosing which emergencies warrant a response. For all these reasons, a policy of proportionate intervention is both necessary and possible for finite agents like us. It is therefore permissible for us to intervene in some cases without thereby automatically acquiring an obligation to intervene in all.

God, on the other hand, has (as far as we have reason to suppose) no such limitations of attention, resources, or compassion. On most versions of personalistic theism, God is compassionately aware of absolutely every case of suffering of every sentient creature, and indeed of each creature's degree and precise qualitative experience of suffering. Where we humans see a clear difference between, on one hand, an emergency that cries out for a dramatic and immediate reaction and, on the other hand, a general state of misery that warrants a longer-term, more subtle, and more gentle response, God sees no such dichotomy but a vast continuum of suffering far more pervasive, intense, and immediate in its need for relief than we could ever allow ourselves to appreciate.[8]

It makes sense, then, to say that human beings can intervene sometimes without being obligated to intervene always, because the occasions and the capacities of human intervention are so drastically limited by our finitude (as well as our sins!). Yet God lacks the luxury of our finitude. God therefore has no reason to intervene in the case of what we regard as unusual suffering while tolerating the less visible suffering that God perceives across the spectrum of sentient life.

But what about "hidden" interventions? Why couldn't God intervene in ways that are not "humanly distinguishable,"[9] so that the world still has the *appearance* of regularity required by the regularity argument above? If this response works, God would not be limited by the not-even-once principle and could act in subtle and diverse ways to reduce suffering—as long as the natural regularities still appeared to hold.

This suggestion faces a few difficulties, however. For one thing, those who would advance this position must admit that God acts to reduce the suffering of some but not others, which means that they attribute to God precisely the inconsistency that Wildman has identified in the quotation with which this chapter began. Further, it's not clear that they avoid the specter of arbitrariness that, we have argued, threatens to undercut science and rational agency. Scientists who endorsed this response would have to say that, although they act *as if* the world were regular and do not expect ever to actually catch God working a miracle, they in fact believe that God is constantly setting aside natural regularities just below the surface of human detection. To believe this is to believe that the natural order is in fact laden with irregularities, however lawlike it may appear to us in practice.

Second response

So far we have been addressing the first of the two questions provoked by our main hypothesis: why can't God at least *sometimes* override the regularities of nature when doing so is needed to prevent innocent suffering? We have answered this question in two ways: first, by showing why the development of rational and autonomous agents requires a greater degree of regularity than might initially be obvious; and second, by arguing that occasional divine abrogations of natural law, even if metaphysically possible, turn out to be morally inconsistent with the capacities of a divine agent—not because breaking natural laws is inherently immoral, but because by doing so God would incur a responsibility to intervene in most or all cases of suffering. But this would make it impossible for God to limit the frequency of such interventions and therefore to preserve a universe in which beings like us could evolve.

But have we now, as the saying goes, "proven too much"? In showing why God cannot intervene in such a way as to suspend the operation of natural regularities, have we also shown that God is unable to act at all within the created universe and therefore that, as

Wildman argues, the personal agency of God is simply irrelevant to human experience and action? This is the second question raised by our hypothesis. In contrast to the first, answering this one will compel us to go beyond the logical implications of the hypothesis itself and to introduce a substantive claim about the nature of the universe in which we happen to find ourselves.

If God is to be able to perform finite actions that bring about events in the created universe—events that would not have occurred merely as a result of the universe's own internal processes—then, given the restrictions on divine agency we have already established, there must be at least one area or sphere of existence within the created universe where events are not determined by the operation of natural regularities. And indeed there is such a sphere of existence: the sphere of thought, or mental activity, or, let us simply say, of mind.

The nonlawlike nature of the mental

Of course, there is no question that mind can play the role we have just suggested if a human being has an immaterial soul that is fundamentally different in kind from the rest of what exists in the natural world. But perhaps one does not have to be a dualist, believing that mind and body are two different kinds of substance, to see how mental events might not be governed by natural laws in the same way physical events are. In this section we present another way to conceive mind, one derived from the study of complex systems in biology, neurology, and cultural studies. Scholars in these fields often use the term "emergent complexity" to describe this approach. (This section, although essential to our argument, is also perhaps the most technical portion of the book. Those who find it heavy going are encouraged to skip ahead to the following section.)

The principles underlying emergent complexity are that there are multiple levels of organization in the natural world, that the way things happen changes radically as one moves upward from one level to the next, and that prediction becomes less and less precise as the systems become more complex. In fact, by the time we get to something as complex as a person or a society, the agents being studied have become so strongly individualized that it becomes questionable whether their actions can still be explained in terms of underlying laws. A technical label for the resulting understanding of persons and their properties is "anomalous monism" (from *a* + *nomos*, hence "not law-governed").[10]

The term "anomalous monism," made famous by the philosopher Donald Davidson, signals the intention of avoiding dualist theories of mind. Dualists, once again, are those who assert the existence of two separate yet interacting substances: mental and physical substances or, more simply, minds and bodies. By contrast, monists maintain that there is only one basic kind of "stuff" in the world; everything that exists is composed of some combination of matter and energy. It seems obvious that mental properties, such as recognizing a differential equation or intending to be funny, are very different sorts of properties from the property of conducting electricity or absorbing oxygen. Still, according to monists, all the diverse properties that we experience and that scientists study are properties of the same basic stuff of which the entire universe is composed.

The adjective "anomalous" signals that mental events are not nomological, that is, not law-based. Although one expects there to be significant patterns and detectible regularities among mental phenomena, those phenomena are not manifestations of some overarching system of laws that govern all mental events. Intentional explanations have irreducibly holistic features; one cannot reduce them to their neurophysiological components without losing the very thing one hopes to explain: the agent's intentions. For example, there are no independent means for specifying what factors are or are not relevant to an intentional act; hence there is no way to link such acts to a specific part of the physical world and to explain them fully in terms of lower-level laws. As Davidson notes, "any effort at increasing the accuracy and power of a theory of behavior forces us to bring more and more of the whole system of the agent's beliefs into account."[11]

Of course, generalizations still can be drawn across many instances of human behavior or across many behaviors of a given individual. Thus we speak of character, dispositions, patterns of behavior, and distinct tendencies manifested by particular groups, societies, and cultures. But there are no grounds for concluding that human behaviors (or, for that matter, behaviors of nonhuman intelligent beings, if any such exist) are merely instantiations of some underlying set of mental or physical laws.[12] Nor does it appear possible to predict complex mental phenomena, such as the next philosophical argument you may construct, on the basis of the equations of physics, biology, or neurology.[13]

We do not here take a position on exactly how constrained or how "free" human actions are. To accept the holism of an "anomalous" account of mind is to maintain that, despite the dependence of the mental on the physical, human actions are not determined by the operation of natural laws or regularities. Yet it is not to deny that such actions manifest significant regularities. Patterns of human action may be law*like*, and rigorous forms of quantitative social science may well be possible. Yet they will not be equivalent to, and hence (in principle) reducible to, natural scientific laws.[14] Nor must one conclude that our mental experiences are merely "epiphenomenal," that is, that they are caused by the firings of neurons in the brain but do not themselves have any causal effects at all on subsequent thought or action.[15]

Now in Davidson's particular case, anomalous monism is wedded to an underlying assumption of physicalism. But does monism *have* to be physicalist? Can one do justice to contemporary science without the assumption that physics (or sciences reducible to physics) can describe fully the nature of what is and what causal forces are operative in the world? Does microphysics have to determine the parameters of one's ontology? As we saw in the previous chapter, recent theories of evolutionary emergence challenge physics-centered accounts of the natural world, offering evidence that each emergent level will require its own explanations and causal descriptions. Theories in ecology or psychology are not unleashed from nature; they must still remain consistent with physical laws. But the leash turns out to be rather longer than one might have thought; emerging structures and functions do much more of the explanatory work than the advocates of reductionism had predicted. What we need is a version of anomalous monism that moves beyond the physicalist assumptions that Davidson built into his particular position.

What then of the criticisms made by some philosophers that science requires one to accept the theory of the causal closure of the physical world (CCP)? CCP asserts that the universe is a closed causal system and that the total amount of energy in the universe is fixed. Of course, if one accepts the view that all sciences (or even all knowledge of any kind) should be reducible to explanations in physics, the costs of *not* accepting CCP are enormous. After all, if all valid scientific knowledge must be expressed in terms of idealized, purely physical systems, then to challenge CCP would be to challenge the possibility of carrying out the computations on which all knowledge ultimately depends.

But it has turned out, we suggest, that reductionist philosophies of science are not able to tell the whole story of scientific knowledge. Different explanatory principles come into play at different levels in the hierarchy of complexity (or, to put this in another way, at different stages in the emergent process of evolution). Although learning more about the interconnections between these levels remains one of the important goals of science, understanding the distinct organizing principles *at each particular level* is also a crucial task. Only at the "lowest" levels of the hierarchy can one rely on models of ideal physical systems that manifest CCP. By the time one begins to study living organisms, for example, the assumption of CCP plays no significant role in day-to-day scientific work. Biological systems require massive inputs of energy or, in technical language, they exist far from thermodynamic equilibrium; in Stuart Kauffman's poetic (but accurate) phrase, they live "at the edge of chaos."[16] Thus biologists never study organisms as closed systems but always in their interactions with their surrounding environments.

In short, we are arguing that the postreductionist or "emergentist" framework is scientifically acceptable and that it does not require the assumption of CCP.[17] Emergent complexity can be studied at any given level of organization. In each case one investigates the causal constraints imposed by lower-level systems and the emergent properties, including causal properties, of the system in question. The same holds for brains and the emergent mental properties that are so crucial for explaining human actions. Affirming the reality and causal roles of thoughts and ideas does not require one to affirm the existence of a separate entity, such as a soul, that acts as an agent to bring about changes in the brain with which it is (somehow) associated. It is enough to suppose that agents with intentions and plans carry out actions in the world. Any adequate explanation will therefore have to include the full range of properties associated with the actions of persons.

Both neurologists and social scientists agree on the role of the broader social environment in affecting brains, ideas, and actions.[18] Ideas like marriage, success, or justice make reference to cultural networks; hence understanding these social realities is crucial for understanding persons and their ideas.[19] It just isn't true that the whole story can be told in neurological terms. The overall psycho-physical state of a person is relevant here—including her social location, her beliefs about herself, and the range of "live options" that are available to her through her culture—because all these are causal factors that affect the physical state of her body. The very chemistry of her neural synapses would be different from what it is if her psychological, mental, and social state were different.[20]

What relevance does this account have to debates about the nature and possibility of divine action? It would be wrong to construe the hypothesis we have outlined here as a proof that divine action is in fact possible. At best, it is a viable answer to the question: is there a way to conceive divine action that is noninterventionist, that breaks no physical laws, and that is consistent with the ongoing pursuit of science?

Suppose that, above the level of the mental, there is a yet higher type of property; call it the spiritual. If the emergentist account of mental causation is correct, then it is possible to apply the same logic to this new level. Just as no natural laws are broken when one explains the behavior of human beings in terms of their thoughts and intentions, so also no laws are broken when one explains human behavior in terms that include the causal influence of spiritual properties on their thinking and consequent actions. (The following argument also works if one construes spiritual properties as part of the mental life.)

Now different people give different accounts of how these spiritual properties are to be interpreted. Biologists might say that they are byproducts of human evolution, and social scientists might explain them in terms of their functions in human social interactions. If one believes that all that exists is the material universe, one will be inclined to explain spiritual properties and ideas as unintended side-effects of mundane realities.

But what if one is convinced by the arguments for the existence of a not-less-than-personal ultimate reality? If such a reality does in fact underlie and permeate this universe, as we have argued, then it would be natural to assume that its effects would be felt at the emergent level or levels that we are calling mental and spiritual.[21] Of course, if the cultural world were a closed physical system, or if all mental and spiritual phenomena were reducible to natural laws, this connection would be impossible. But we have argued that both assumptions are mistaken. It follows that scientists and philosophers who accept the emergence of mental properties can accept at least the possibility that the divine "lure" operates at this level.

An emergentist theory of mind thus opens up the possibility of a divine influence at the mental or spiritual level that does not require an exception to any natural laws. But could a critic now use this conclusion to undercut the not-even-once principle that forms the core of our response to the argument from neglect? After all, if human mental life can have some effect on the underlying neurophysiological structures on which it is dependent, why couldn't God—whom we also assume to have mental properties—*also* directly cause changes in the physical world?

The answer to this challenge lies in a fundamental assumption of the emergentist position: the regularities in nature that we call natural laws. To grant that mental activity is anomalous (that is, not law-governed) is not to ignore the more ordered systems on which such activity depends. Indeed, it is only thanks to these natural regularities that scientists are able to study the various levels of emergent complexity in the first place.

The theory of emergence assumes, in other words, that there are important continuities across contiguous levels of the natural world. Chemical properties emerge from physical systems, attributes that we associate with life are holistic properties of living systems (cells and groups of cells), and basic mental properties are predicated of brains and the persons who have them rather than of an immaterial human soul. Emergent complexity can play a role within scientific research programs only as long as the causal relations in each case can be reconstructed and studied. In cases where lower-level explanations are not by themselves sufficient, empirical reasons can be given (e.g., bifurcations, phase transitions, system effects) for introducing a new explanatory level. In every case, the result is a particular field of empirical study, and the seamlessness of natural explanation is preserved.

So a theory of emergent mental causation does not support the notion of direct divine influence on the domains of (say) physics or chemistry. During most of evolution, emergence took place between contiguous levels of lawlike phenomena, supporting an impressive continuity of explanation. At a certain point in the process of emergence, however, there arose phenomena and entities, such as persons, whose behavior could no longer be explained by subsuming it under general laws. At that point it became possible for divine agency—which is certainly not dependent on, or even contiguous with, any lower level of reality—to exert its influence, yet to do so without undercutting the conditions that make scientific explanations possible in the many domains to which they apply.

We have argued in this section that the sphere of mental activity is one area of existence in which God can act without incurring an obligation to prevent events like the Asian tsunami. We have also suggested that, if there are any emergent levels above the mental, they would be open to divine influence in a similar way. But is such influence ever possible *below* that level? Might it be, for example, that there are other phenomena in the biosphere that have "anomalous" features, features sufficiently similar to the anomalous nature of human mental functioning that divine influence might operate there as well?

Answering these questions means sifting through complex empirical and conceptual material in the biological sciences and would require a much longer presentation. One should note, however, that the position we have defended would allow for divine influence on organisms prior to *Homo sapiens* as long as the same conditions were met. It then becomes an empirical rather than a philosophical question whether these conditions are actually met elsewhere in the universe. Our sole aim here has been to show that the realm of the mental represents at least one natural sphere in which divine action can occur, without overriding the regularities whose preservation is a necessary condition for the emergence of finite rational agents.

Does the problem of evil now return in a new form?

Suppose all this is correct. Suppose it is indeed the case that God can perform intentional acts of communication with the minds of those creatures who are capable of receiving what God conveys. Are we not faced, once again, with Wildman's "argument from neglect"? It isn't as if a divine agent could only prevent innocent suffering by performing physical miracles, such as stopping or reconfiguring the seismic movement that caused the December 2004 tsunami. Why would a benevolent God have refrained from somehow warning those in its path that the wave was on its way?

The tsunami example, tragic as it is, is perhaps worth dwelling on. After all, our whole account entails the existence of a God who, on one hand, refrains from altering the regularity of natural processes and, on the other hand, performs purposeful actions in and through the thoughts of human beings. Unless we suppose that God's refusal to interfere with physical processes entails that God is simply unaware of those processes, we have to assume that God knew instantly that the Sumatra–Andaman earthquake had occurred, even if this was (on some accounts) something God could not have known ahead of time. But even if one were to suppose that God was unaware of physical events like undersea earthquakes, the very hypothesis that God performs acts of communication with human minds entails that God is aware of what human beings think, say, and experience; and that entails, for instance, that God must have known the tsunami was headed for Sri Lanka within moments of its striking Sumatra.

Assuming, then, that God knew about the impending disaster in Sri Lanka some two hours before it occurred, how do we explain why so many thousands of Sri Lankans (and their visitors) continued to work and play along the beaches without, apparently, the slightest hint that death was on its way? Should we say, for instance, that God is aware of our thoughts but can't perform the inferences we can and therefore could not extrapolate from the wave's hitting Sumatra that it must be on its way to Sri Lanka as well? Or should we suggest instead that God is aware of our thoughts but, lacking our referential framework, is simply unable to *understand* our thoughts? But if either of these speculations is true, it becomes hard to see how one can claim that God is capable of performing purposeful acts of communication with human minds.

We seem to face a dilemma. The critic of personal theism has argued that if all divine action is impossible, God becomes "virtually irrelevant" to human action. And yet if God were to intervene in such a way as to impart information that, directly and inescapably, affected an individual's psychological state—for instance, by conveying an unambiguous warning of an impending disaster—then God would be obliged to intervene in every case in which an intervention of this kind would yield a better outcome. In other words, either God is capable of conveying information to human minds, in which case God's failure to do so in a situation like that of the tsunami leaves the theist defenseless against the argument from neglect; or divine and human thoughts are so incommensurable, and hence so mutually untranslatable, that we are compelled to abandon any meaningful notion of communication between God and human minds.

Formulating this dilemma helps to clarify both the logic and the limitations of the argument we have been making. It points first to the intentionally formal nature of the account of divine action we have been providing. The truth is that one cannot infer from general constraints of the sort we have explored what *specific* constraints might apply to divine action in any given instance. Indeed, even to imagine God as carefully observing some set of constraints in order to decide how and when to act is to conceive divine agency in an overly anthropomorphic way. From that point of view, what we have described as the not-even-once principle is more accurately conceived as pointing to a structural feature of divine–human interaction, not a moral obligation that God must strive to fulfill.

With that clarification in mind, however, the question remains: if the content of divine communication is not such that it could be used to warn human beings of imminent danger, what kind of content might it be? Perhaps divine communication takes an *axiological* form, where God presents to a person's consciousness a value that she is free to embrace, pursue, reject, or ignore. Or perhaps it goes beyond communication per se, taking the form of God's bringing about the kind of religious experience in which the subject becomes aware of God's presence. In fact, those two kinds of action might be combined, we suggest, in the form of an experience in which a sense of the divine presence leads to an apprehension of axiological truths, and also fosters, perhaps, the courage to act on them.[22]

Perhaps an example will help to clarify how axiological communication can occur without providing the kind of information that raises the problem of evil. Consider the case of a medical technician who unwittingly prepares a fatal overdose of what would otherwise have been a life-saving medicine, because he failed to pay close enough attention to the placement of a decimal point in the physician's hastily composed instructions. God might have prevented this accident in countless ways, for instance by placing in the technician's mind a command to double-check the prescription; or perhaps by causing him to feel intensely anxious at some appropriate juncture in the act of measuring out the dosage. Had the technician ignored either of these divine signals, God could have responded by, as it were, turning up the volume, until the technician was left with no choice but to comply!

In these and no doubt innumerable other ways, once again, God could intentionally act in the mind of a finite agent to prevent an error from having its fatal effect. But if God were to do so, the objector to personal theism would correctly point out, God would thereby incur an obligation to intervene in similar ways whenever a human failing was about to have disastrous consequences. The result would be a negation of finite rational agency at least as complete as the negation that would result from continual divine intervention in the sphere of physical events. By contrast, God could present to an agent the general value of being careful as an expression of love for one's neighbor, and the agent would be free to embrace, or not to embrace, that value as a component of her motivational set.[23] In that case, no negation of finite agency would occur.

As this example shows, what matters is not so much the precise mode of divine communication as whether the effects of divine action, communicative or otherwise, are mediated through the agency of the individual with whom God interacts. What God cannot do, if the problem of evil is to be answerable, is to give us thoughts or feelings that compel an automatic or reflexive response, because if that was the way God acted in the world, God would have an obligation to prevent or correct our mistakes and other failures whenever they might occur. But a world in which mistakes were impossible would be a world in which finite rational agency was also impossible.

Theories of divine action are, by the nature of the case, speculative and uncertain. Still, our results do point unambiguously *away* from certain claims, such as the claim that God directly compels human actions or conveys inescapable knowledge of specific truths to human minds. Now that we have a sense of what a theory of divine action *cannot* include, it becomes possible to sketch at least the outlines of a plausible theory of what it might involve, which we will call *a participatory theory of divine–human agency.*

It is not correct, it turns out, to say that a specific divine content (say, a set of clearly stated, divinely authorized propositions) is imparted by God and subsequently interpreted by human agents.[24] But nor is one forced to conclude that there is no divine input whatsoever, only the evolving beliefs of human agents.[25] The alternative is to suppose that God continually lures all of creation to conformity with the divine nature. Given the view of God we have arrived at, this divine attraction does not need to be understood as impersonal, like the force of magnetism, nor as a universal message offering the same content to all agents, as if it were a kind of divine radio broadcast. Instead, it is possible that the lure is highly differentiated, calling different individuals to different types of action or response. The problem of evil, however, has made clear that the message to each agent cannot arrive fully formed and formulated, as if each person needed only to turn on her inner receiver to know precisely what God would have her do. Instead, it is a lure that only becomes a definite message as it is interpreted and formulated by each recipient. Nor does the fact that interpretation is involved mean that the resulting content is "merely" a product of human invention.

This theory of divine action assumes an infinite divine–human asymmetry. God preexisted the universe and initiated the processes and the specific conditions that produced all living things, including human beings. God also precedes every instance of divine interaction with each human being and, one can assume, apprehends much more in the interaction than human agents do. God is always luring, and humans are always responding, although the responses may not be conscious. There is no conceptual difficulty in supposing that every instance of divine–human interaction involves a combination of divine and human contributions, even if it is impossible to isolate the divine input from its human interpretation. Indeed, on the assumption that a genuinely dialectical fusion of agency occurs, one knows in advance that it will be impossible to analyze exactly how and where the various components come together. From what vantage point, after all, could a finite human being isolate her own specific contribution to what emerges through her interaction with an infinite agent whose agency always precedes, envelops, and pervades her own agency?

There is no reliable way, then, to separate the divine from the human contributions to any particular instance of divine–human interaction. That doesn't prevent one from judging, however, that one sometimes perceives the divine will more clearly than at other times, or that some persons live more fully than others in accordance with divine values (and hence with the divine "will"). At the highest end of this continuum stands the possibility of a perfect fusion of divine and human wills, producing what amounts to a single will and agency out of the contributions of two separate agents. This dialectical fusion of agency remains as an ideal even if it is rarely achieved, and even if *all* actions include a divine and a human component. We return to this ideal in Chapter 6.

As we noted above, this account presupposes an emergentist understanding of cosmic evolution and of mind.[26] It also conceives the relationship between God and finite agents after the fashion of *panentheism*, which is the view that the world is contained within the divine although God is also more than the world.[27] For panentheists, every action, since it takes place "within" the divine, represents an act of God in some sense. The dialectical understanding of human agency that panentheists endorse has important implications for conceiving human freedom, rationality, the knowability of God, and religious pluralism, among other topics.[28]

In combining these two contemporary schools of thought—panentheism and emergence theory—we arrive at an understanding of divine–human interaction in which each side of the relationship must in some degree anticipate the other, even if the process presupposes an original divine anticipation and therefore an asymmetry between divine and human agencies. After all, the sort of communication we have described between God and finite agents becomes fully possible only at the point where evolution has produced organisms capable of personal interaction. At the same time, however, panentheists believe that this emergent intentionality already participates from its inception in the intentionality of God; it thus anticipates whatever communication from God finite beings will eventually be capable of comprehending. For that reason, each particular instance of divine influence is always a response to what is already present in the being God influences. It must take into account the particular beings and the particular properties that have emerged up to that point in the evolutionary process.

By constraining divine agency in the way the participatory theory suggests, have we once again impaled ourselves on the second horn of Wildman's dilemma? Have we reduced the scope and efficacy of divine action to the point where it indeed becomes irrelevant to human moral struggles? We contend that we have not. For on our account, not only has God purposely created a universe in which there could evolve beings capable of making moral choices and entering into communion with God. God also purposely and graciously responds to, and interacts with, those beings, accompanying them on their journeys, inspiring their joys, and luring them, gently, into harmony with the divine will.

Is all of that "virtually irrelevant" to our moral struggles, as Wildman argues? Does moral relevance consist only in the power to perform dramatic acts of intervention? If so, not only is God morally irrelevant; so are all the great moral exemplars of the past who, being dead, are even more powerless to act on behalf of justice!

God, on the hypothesis we have been exploring, is not only the creator of the natural regularities that enable finite moral agents to exist in the first place; God is also engaged with us, once again, in the modes of gentle guidance, growing illumination, and persistent attraction. Such a God may not be able to stop a fatal mudslide, or warn the villagers of its impending arrival. But it by no means follows that such a God is morally irrelevant.

On the contrary: a participatory conception of divine–human interaction suggests that God is involved in every instance of human action and experience in ways that infinitely exceed our comprehension. And that provides an opportunity to prevent a certain misunderstanding that can easily result from responses to the argument from neglect—and more broadly, the problem of evil—of the kind we have developed here. When we propose that God's permitting innocent suffering is a necessary consequence of God's creating a universe in which autonomous beings can evolve, it might seem that we are engaging in the kind of Leibnizian calculation—justifying the existence of suffering by weighing it against some overriding set of good outcomes—that has long given theodicy a bad name. On that scenario, an impassive God considers whether to create a universe with a certain ratio of good and evil and is justified in proceeding if the former exceeds the latter. And to that scenario, Dostoevsky's Ivan and Alyosha Karamazov have surely given the final and unanswerable reply:

"Tell me yourself, I challenge you—answer. Imagine that you are creating a fabric of human destiny with the object of making men happy in the end, giving them peace and rest at last, but that it was essential and inevitable to torture to death only one tiny creature—that baby beating its breast with its fist, for instance—and to found that edifice on its unavenged tears, would you consent to be the architect on those conditions? Tell me, and tell the truth."

"No, I wouldn't consent," said Alyosha softly.[29]

The situation changes, however, if the motive of creation is, as we suggested in Chapter 2, nothing more or less than God's self-emptying love for that which is other than God's self, and if genuine otherness can only exist if there is a world where suffering is real. The situation changes still further if one has reason to think that suffering is not a phenomenon that God abstractly contemplates but a reality in which God participates with a degree of comprehensiveness and intimacy that, once again, exceeds our imagination.

The eschatological dimension

We have another response, however, to the second prong of the argument from neglect. If, despite all that we have argued, Wildman's argument should turn out to be correct after all, and if one were forced to the conclusion that God was not a personal agent, what would one have to say about the moral relevance of theism in what would then be its nonpersonal form?

At the very least, it seems to us that the moral relevance of this version of theism would tend to be confined to those who already, as the Gospel saying goes, "have their reward." It might in various ways inspire the small minority of those with leisure to contemplate the faceless mystery it posits. But if God has not acted to create a universe containing finite persons about whose future God cares—say, because God is incapable of acting or caring at all—then suffering in this life, and indeed the fate of the vast majority of all human beings who have ever lived, is unredeemed and unredeemable, and their hope is not only false but cruel. There can be no hope of any future consummation. It seems a not unreasonable *tu quoque* to ask the arguer from neglect about the moral contribution of such despair to "the practical moral struggles of our deeply unjust world."

Evoking the hope of an eschatological fulfillment, however, raises one final possible objection to the somewhat minimalistic picture of divine agency that we have developed, partly although not exclusively in response to the argument from neglect. If innocent suffering is a necessary part of a universe in which rational and autonomous agents can evolve, and if God for good reason refrains from preventing it, why should we suppose that God has the power or disposition to bring about a different "cosmological epoch" in which innocent suffering would be absent? In correspondence with the authors, Wesley Wildman (source of the phrase just quoted) has posed this challenge in the following lucid terms:

... God's nature[,] including morally relevant aspects of God's nature[,] must be consistent across all cosmological epochs because of your view of divine creation. Pictures of that nature derived from one epoch must be relevant somehow to all epochs, accordingly. If God can and does act in a way you approve in a cosmological epoch you want to imagine but don't actually live in, then God should be able to do that in this cosmological epoch, also, on pain of moral inconsistency.

This is a powerful objection, among other reasons because the need to preserve God's moral consistency has played so crucial a role in our response to the argument from neglect. We appear to face one final dilemma: we can either give up the notion that God is morally consistent, thereby jettisoning our explanation of why God cannot at least *occasionally* intervene to prevent innocent suffering; or give up the notion of different cosmological epochs, at the cost of undermining the plausibility of our claim that God seeks communion with finite persons.

Is it clear, however, that God's altering the conditions of finite existence in a later cosmological epoch would entail the kind of moral inconsistency Wildman supposes? What if God has a good reason to alter the conditions of finite existence between this and a subsequent epoch, precisely because so doing is the best way of realizing God's overarching moral purpose? On the hypothesis we have been developing and defending throughout this chapter, God's ultimate purpose is to bring about the existence of finite persons with the capacity to enter freely into a loving fellowship with God. Again on our hypothesis, persons fitting that description can only come into existence if they are not simply projections of the divine will but have emerged from a process designed to endow them with (relative) autonomy.[30]

According to John Hick, who employed a similar approach in his early book *Evil and the God of Love*, it is reasonable to suppose that such a process would have to continue in worlds beyond this one (because so many persons in this world lack the opportunity to develop morally and religiously at all, or to develop as fully as God would presumably desire that they should), and this future epoch (or these epochs) would indeed exhibit conditions identical or at least functionally similar to the ones that cause suffering in ours. Perhaps the process of development is never-ending, and God's actions in all future epochs are restricted by the very same considerations that restrict them in this one, although the persons who move through those successive worlds continue to grow in their love of God and neighbor. Or it could be that, in the next epoch (or perhaps at the end of a very long succession), each person reaches a stage where further "soul-making" (in Hick's Keatsian phrase) is no longer needed, at which point she may enter an epoch with an entirely different set of cosmological conditions.[31]

Again, the underlying assumption here is that God has "in mind" the same desideratum across however many epochs it takes to develop persons to the point to which God intends that they develop. Across all these epochs, divine action is limited only by the cosmological constraints required to produce and sustain autonomous persons. It is not obvious that the conditions necessary for a world in which autonomous persons can develop (i.e., the conditions necessary for *this* world) are also necessary for a future world in which fully developed persons can flourish in the communion for which they were intended. Hence the evils inherent in this world might not be entailed by the next.

In short, it is perfectly possible for God to create other and better worlds without contradicting what, on our hypothesis, was God's purpose in creating this one. And that hypothesis, we submit, provides a sufficiently plausible answer to the argument from neglect.

4

The plurality of religions

I n the foregoing chapters, we have presented a certain vision of the ultimate reality (UR), a vision in which that reality is personal—or as we would prefer to say, not *less* than personal—and manifests the kind of other-directed action in creation that, in the human context, one would call love. In Chapter 3, we responded to one important challenge to that vision, arising from what is traditionally known as the "problem of evil." We defended the claim that, despite the existence of innocent suffering, the UR could still be seen as a God who responded with compassion toward finite creatures. This required us to provide a plausible explanation of the apparent absence of divine action in situations where one might expect it to occur. That explanation came at a certain cost: direct divine intervention was absent in such situations, we suggested, because God could not act, even once, in ways that would be incompatible with the regularities we call the laws of nature without becoming obligated to act in all cases where a similar good would be produced. That still left room for a kind of divine action we called "participatory" because it involved God's acting in and through the agency of finite beings, and doing so in a way that did not negate the relative autonomy of those finite beings themselves.

The overall picture that has emerged from these earlier chapters amounts to a hypothesis—it cannot be more than that—about what is ultimately the case: what really obtains, in the last analysis, beyond all the profound and startling discoveries of natural science, and beneath the chaotic events of cosmic, biological, and cultural evolution. The hypothesis itself is a complex one; it is not of a kind that can be tested in a laboratory or proven with logical arguments that will persuade all reasonable persons who examine them. Nevertheless, we think it makes sense to regard this picture of the UR as better than the alternatives.

Those alternatives, incidentally, are exactly four in number: first, that the universe is both eternal (it has no origin) and necessary (it could not *not* have existed, hence it is self-explanatory);[1] second, that the ultimate and only origin of the universe was a random quantum fluctuation in the void or some other entirely mindless and impersonal process; third, that the universe was the creation of a personal being but one who happens to be either hostile or indifferent to finite persons and what matters to them; and, fourth, that there is simply no meaningful answer to the question of what is ultimately the case or why there is anything at all.

There are certainly considerations that might incline a reasonable person to choose one of these alternatives over ours. But we have tried to show why, even in the light of problems as challenging as the one addressed in Chapter 3, it makes more sense to suppose that the source and ground of all existence is an infinite reality more aptly described as personal than impersonal, and better conceived as valuing the welfare of its finite creatures than as hostile or indifferent to them. It also makes sense to suppose that this infinite being will be disposed to perform certain kinds of actions within the finite universe, insofar as such actions are compatible with the relative autonomy that, we argue, the universe must have if it is to sustain the evolutionary emergence of finite persons.

And that, we submit, is about as far as metaphysical reflection can go. Remember that metaphysics is reflection based on general scientific principles and philosophical arguments, reflection that does not appeal to the contingent facts of history. The results of such reflection remain unsatisfyingly abstract. They do not help one determine which human values, beyond a general altruism, in fact characterize the UR, or which events in the course of human history have been shaped, and to what degree, by the influence of whatever participatory communicative actions the UR may have performed.

In short, the implications of our theory—call it *minimally personalistic theism* or MPT—stop well shy of yielding the kinds of concrete claims about historical events and moral laws that form the intellectual framework of human religions. After all, most religious traditions make highly concrete claims about what human beings should believe regarding the nature of the UR and what they should do in response to it.[2]

The hypothesis we have developed in the foregoing chapters operates at too high an altitude, then, to be of much direct religious interest or usefulness. As our use of the term "God" suggests, it clearly does *point* in a religious direction, by raising the question of whether any sort of worshipful or practical response ought to follow from what we can infer about the ultimate source and purpose of the universe in which human beings find themselves. In that sense, the previous chapters may be religiously suggestive, but their conclusions evaporate, so to speak, before they reach the religious ground.

At the same time, however, the kind of reflection contained in the first three chapters is not typical of what generally goes under the name "metaphysics" today, either on "metaphysics" shelves in bookstores or in textbooks in analytic philosophy.[3] Recall how we were led to this type of reflection. As we thought about the metaphysical implications of contemporary science, we found ourselves confronted with the question of what kind of UR might have preceded the universe as a whole. These topics led us in turn to the central issues of philosophical theism: is this not-less-than-personal ultimate what we would call good, or is it indifferent to our moral concerns? Does suffering in the world undercut belief in such a reality? Clearly, once metaphysical reflection leads to a personal ultimate, metaphysics begins to shade over into philosophy of religion, and even to implicitly theological topics.

At that point, however, one encounters a major methodological break. Perhaps surprisingly, this break does not come with the transition to theism; it comes when one turns from theism in general to the specific historical and doctrinal beliefs of the individual religions. For the path of reflection now forces us to pose a question that seems as difficult to avoid as it appears impossible to answer: where, if anywhere, in human history does one find signs of the presence and activity of an ultimate reality one has reason to regard as more like a personal agent than an impersonal force?

The problem is that, even if one accepts the case we have been making for minimally personal theism, MPT itself seems to offer insufficient reason to choose among the many religious options that potentially claim one's attention, and perhaps one's allegiance, in to-day's radically globalized religious environment. There are some options, of course, that MPT rules out. Those include nontheistic religions that regard the UR as impersonal or unknowable; equally, theistic religions that proclaim a God who actively intervenes to alter what would otherwise be the natural course of physical events. But there remains a broad range of religious traditions that share enough of the core elements of MPT that they are in many ways surprisingly similar. Those very similarities prevent one from using MPT to choose among them when their claims conflict.

Consider, first, the similarities. Historically, Jews, Christians, and Muslims share a common belief in the God of the Hebrew Bible. Many core beliefs about that God are endorsed by all three of these "Abrahamic faiths."[4] The philosophical and theological development of this notion of God likewise involved frequent cross-fertilization among these traditional faiths. At the beginning of the Common Era, Philo Judaeus, also known as Philo of Alexandria (20 BCE to 50 CE), first synthesized Greek metaphysical concepts with the notion of God advanced in the Hebrew Bible, and later theologians in all three traditions built upon the conceptual foundations he laid down. Maimonides' work played a similar role for the theologies of the medieval period, exerting a vast influence on Muslim and Christian thought (see, for instance, the frequent citations of "Rabbi Moses" in Thomas Aquinas's *Summa theologiae*). In the high Middle Ages, exchanges among Jewish, Christian, and Muslim thinkers were crucial to the development of all three traditions. For example, theological conclusions from the Islamic philosophers Ibn Sina (Avicenna), Ibn Rushd (Averroes), and Al-Ghazali had a major impact on subsequent Jewish and Christian theology.

The movement of "scriptural reasoning" in recent years has increased the sense of a common scriptural basis for these notions of God.[5] In contemporary theology, moreover, one finds a variety of more specific parallels among the faith traditions. For example, the Kabbalistic understanding of creation and the God–world relation, with its notion of creation as taking place *within* God, has influenced recent Christian affirmations of panentheism, the view (invoked in Chapter 3) that the world exists within God, although God is also more than the world.[6] The ethical turn in Jewish notions of God in the late nineteenth century (Cohen, Rosenzweig) is matched by a similar ethical shift in twentieth-century Christian thought (Rauschenbusch, the "social gospel" movement, liberation theologies, and much contemporary liberal theology). This list of examples could be extended at will.[7]

Nor are the similarities limited to the Abrahamic faiths. The parallels between Western theism and Hinduism are also closer than is often recognized. The philosophy of Sankara (*c.* 800 CE) connects closely with the "apophatic" theologies in the Western monotheistic religions, which assert that God is beyond all predication, that is, beyond any positive assertions about God that human beings can make. The Hindu Vedantic traditions also show close parallels with Plotinus, Pseudo-Dionysius, and the Neoplatonic tradition in the West. Rāmānuja and the devotional (*bhakti*) tradition in India stand surprisingly close to various traditions of theistic worship in Judaism, Christianity, and Islam. Here consciousness or awareness serves as the basic feature of the divine, as it does in many forms of personalistic theism in the West. Moreover, in the Hindu devotional tradition God is said to be known through worship and inner experience, as also in many Western traditions (e.g., the German liberal tradition initiated by Friedrich Schleiermacher).

Despite all these parallels, it remains the case that the world's religions provide a number of different and (it would seem) not fully compatible ways of pinning down the otherwise very general and abstract content of MPT. The very fact that there are so many conflicting religious theories, all purporting to describe the same UR, provides a powerful *prima facie* reason for doubting that any one of them is more likely to be true than false (see Chapter 1). Reasons for doubt intensify when one realizes that nearly all those who adhere to one religious tradition or another do so because that was the tradition in which they were raised or to which they were heavily exposed by the culture surrounding them.

Moreover, each tradition provides its adherents with compelling experiences that naturally seem to them to confirm the truth of whatever religious theories the tradition may embody. One cannot deny the joy that radiates from the faces of Hindu believers celebrating the festival of Diwali; the deep sense of meaning and purpose that permeates the life of a Jew who strives to obey the 613 *mizvot* of biblical law; the profound spiritual focus that Muslims experience in orienting their life around the five pillars of Islam; or the feelings of peace and confidence that flow from the compassionate ministrations of a Christian Sister of Mercy. Of course there are those who doubt the genuineness of all such experiences, but their skepticism does not alter that fact that, for the believer, the experience tends to confirm the rightness of the religious path on which she finds herself. Yet this only makes the question of religious truth all the more difficult to answer, because an adherent of any single religion must acknowledge, if she is honest, that her experiences would have been entirely different if she had been raised in one of the other traditions.[8]

What conclusion should we draw from the undeniable fact of religious plurality? How serious are the doubts it raises regarding the probability that any particular religious theory is actually true? In recent years, theologians and philosophers of religion have offered a fairly broad range of mutually exclusive answers. John Hick regards every religious theory as a "myth," by which he means a particular story that human beings have invented to depict a reality that lies utterly beyond the reach of human knowledge. (For Hick, metaphysical theories are just as problematic as religious ones, so that MPT itself would count as a myth in his sense of the word.)[9] Others would argue that each religion—or at least each of the major ones—captures a portion of a single truth that, in its totality, transcends the grasp of any particular tradition.[10] Still another option, associated with the work of Alvin Plantinga and other proponents of "Reformed Epistemology," is to admit the fact of religious plurality but deny its relevance, on the grounds that everyone is entitled to hold the beliefs she finds herself holding, unless she encounters unanswerable objections or "defeaters" that properly convince her she is mistaken. On this view, the mere fact that someone holds a different view from mine doesn't matter unless I acquire a "defeater," that is, a positive reason to think that the other person may actually be right.[11]

Then there are arguments like those of Richard Swinburne, who denies our premise that there is no way to get from a general account of the UR to the choice of a particular religion. For Swinburne, there is an unbroken chain of inference from metaphysics to the assessment of conflicting religious testimonies, so that once one has established the probable nature of the UR one can continue to employ philosophical arguments in much the same way, until one is eventually able to establish the truth of complex Christian claims about divine revelation, atonement, and the resurrection of Jesus.[12] A different response emerges from the work of the great Roman Catholic theologian Karl Rahner, who argues that the altruism and hope embodied in the other major religions make them implicitly or, as he says, "anonymously" Christian.[13]

When one steps back from this set of alternatives, they seem to boil down in the end to two basic options. Either the fact of religious plurality shows that there is no answer (or at least no humanly accessible answer) to the question of which, if any, of the available religious alternatives best reflects the nature and intentions of the UR; or else religious plurality is irrelevant to the question of whether the theories embedded in one's own religious tradition are actually true. According to proponents of the first option, there is simply no way around the fact that each of us is trapped in, and indeed essentially blinded by, the religious and cultural milieu in which she happens to find herself. On the second option, religious truth is no more affected by the existence of multiple religions than scientific truth is affected by the fact that people in earlier times believed that the earth was flat. And, many people say, *tertium non datur*: there is no third choice.

But is this really true? Must one really opt for one side or the other? We suggest a somewhat more complex response. In the first place, it seems to us that the existence of other religions *should* reduce one's confidence in the theories embedded in whatever religious tradition one happens to have inherited. This is not like the astronomical case, where one has a theory of error explaining why it seemed to people in former eras that the sun revolved around the earth.[14] The most obvious explanation of the fact that other people believe religious theories other than one's own is not that they are interpreting the same experiences in different (and mistaken) ways but rather that they have had experiences within their traditions to which one has not oneself had access. In other words, particular beliefs about the UR vary with the religious experiences and assumptions (or other tradition-based experiences and assumptions) of those holding those beliefs. The general considerations we canvassed in earlier chapters do not provide any help in deciding which among *these sorts* of beliefs are correct. In that sense, the choice among competing religious theories about the UR is *underdetermined*—left unresolved—by the arguments and the evidence available to the community of inquiry as a whole.

Does it follow that one should simply suspend belief in all particular religious theories, remaining agnostic about any claims that go beyond the generality of a minimally personalistic theism? Does it follow, in other words, that, when it comes to religion, there is simply no truth of the matter, because all religious theories are merely myths or stories that human beings tell themselves about what is ultimately the case?

In our view, this does not follow. In most cases, an essential part of what makes a religion interesting to those who adhere to it is precisely its claim to embody a true account of the nature and intentions of the divine reality to which it responds. The claim that all religions are equally true amounts to the claim that they are equally false, and therefore equally irrelevant to the question of how best to engage the reality they claim to be about.[15] Many, perhaps even most of those who have followed our argument to this point are likely to approach the question of ultimacy from a point of view that has been powerfully shaped by religious experiences that seem to them to support a particular way of understanding and engaging the UR. Even if they grant— as we believe they should—that there are no arguments or evidence that can or should compel others to agree with them, they are not for that reason required to abandon their belief in what their experience inclines them to believe.

To see why, consider the case of Rachel, who witnesses a crime and then discovers that someone else who also witnessed it offers a sharply conflicting account of what occurred. Rachel may well agree that the community of inquiry investigating this case—the jury, let us say— has no reason to reject the other person's testimony in favor of hers. She may agree, in other words, that the choice between the two conflicting accounts is underdetermined by the evidence available to the jury, which was not there to experience what *either* witness experienced.

Should Rachel therefore stop believing what she thinks she saw? Clearly not. She may be frustrated by her inability to convince the jury of her point of view, even while acknowledging that the jury, given the evidence available to it, is right to withhold its assent. And she may or may not be sufficiently puzzled by the difference between her experience and the other witness's account that she is led to doubt her interpretation of her own experience. She *should* acknowledge that her position would be stronger if she had other evidence or arguments that confirmed what she thinks she saw. But—and this point is crucial to the motivation of our next two chapters—she is not compelled to abandon her belief in what she saw, and indeed she is justified in continuing to believe it, unless and until she acquires a reason to think that she was probably mistaken. Disagreement, simply by itself, does not constitute such a reason.

Exactly the same principles apply in the case of religious theories and their relation to the religious experience of those who hold them. If my own experience leads me to interpret the UR in a way that conflicts with the interpretations of those with different experiences, I should acknowledge that the community of religious inquirers has no reason to prefer my theory to theirs. But it doesn't follow that I have a rational duty to stop believing in the reality I think my experience enables me to see.

How, in that case, should one proceed? Some, who stand outside the sphere of religious experience per se, will rightly respond that they will *not* proceed but will stop exactly at this point in our narrative—with reasons to affirm the overall preferability of MPT to its meta-physical alternatives but with no way to assess the more specific claims of any particular religion. To those readers, we can only offer thanks for accompanying us as far as they have; we have no argument that would or should persuade them to go further (unless, of course, they are curious about what may follow from certain assumptions they do not themselves share). Others, by contrast, will just as rightly proceed to explore and evaluate the content and implications of what their experience inclines them to believe. They should not expect their philosophical discussion partners to accept their religious experiences as a substitute for philosophical arguments. But it doesn't follow from this fact that it is unreasonable for *them* to consider their experience when evaluating their own religious tradition. (In Chapter 7 we explore in greater detail what it *is* reasonable for such persons to believe.)

In the following two chapters, we will present a detailed example of an exploration of this kind. In so doing, we will necessarily focus on the interpretation of the UR to which we ourselves are drawn by the nature and content of our own experience. For those whose experi-ence leads them to a different interpretation, our example may suggest analogous ways of proceeding as they consider the claims of their own respective traditions.

To all, we owe a warning. The argument from this point on will necessarily shift gears in a way that will increase the particularity of its claims but, at the same time, diminish the degree to which we can regard those claims as rationally compelling. Until now, our reflections have been based on quite general features of the universe as modern science interprets it, as well as on certain general aspects of human moral experience. In the next two chapters, however, we will turn from the implications of human experience in general to a particular slice of human history; more exactly, to a particular body of testimony about a particular set of human events. Although this loss of universality may be regrettable to some, we maintain that one cannot evaluate the concrete claims of the specific religions—at least in the case of Christianity, and presumably in many of the other traditions as well— without making this shift.

In one sense, the task becomes easier as we descend from the rarefied atmosphere of broadly metaphysical arguments to specific historical claims. But in another sense, the uncertainty that invariably accompanies metaphysical inquiry is necessarily increased when one tries to apply metaphysical conclusions to the interpretation of a reported set of events. The controversies inherent in the metaphysical questions are now compounded by debates about the origin, reliability, and best way of interpreting the testimony that is our only source of access to those events, and our only basis for assessing their possible relevance to the ultimate reality.

5

The scandal of particularity, Part I

The resurrection testimony

Religious pluralism and Christian revelation claims

We have now arrived at the heart of the predicament this book was designed to address. So far we have offered quite general arguments, based on assumptions we hoped would be shared by people of reason and good will across the spectrum of religious, nonreligious, and even antireligious opinion. At every stage of the exposition so far, we have been careful not to rely on the claims of any particular religious tradition, or on the particular experiences and perceptions that one might have as a participant in one as opposed to another tradition.

Of course the generality of that approach does not ensure, or even make it likely, that all readers, wherever they fall on the spectrum of belief and nonbelief, will have accepted the conclusions defended so far in these pages. Those committed to certain kinds of philosophical naturalism will probably continue to reject the notion that the ultimate reality (UR) is not less than personal, while those who accept the occurrence of miracles will no doubt resist the degree to which our account restricts the scope and visibility of divine action. A reader who agrees with us will regard these other readers as mistaken, but that disagreement will not be based on her commitment to a particular framework of religious belief or experience. On the contrary, it will seem to her that they are mistaken, if they are, because they have not yet accepted the consequences of assumptions *to which they themselves are committed*. (It is also possible that they will eventually convince her that it is we, not they, who have misunderstood the implications of the assumptions they and we share.)

In any case, the conclusions we have reached at this level of generality are noticeably thin; one may justifiably complain that they are not substantial enough to fuel a successful religious life (certainly not a traditional one!) or a vibrant religious community. We have reason to think that the UR is not less than personal, but that tells us nothing about what kind of personal, or more than personal, reality the UR actually is. We have reason to suppose the UR—or God, as we may call it, once its not-less-than-personal nature has been established—may share at least some of our values, but that gives us no help in deciding which ones, or whether God would approve of the way we pursue them. We have reason to think that God communicates with human beings, but that assumption offers no help in deciding when or what God communicates.

Have we therefore arrived at the end of what can be said to, and assessed by, a general audience? Have we reached the point at which the only way to move forward is to enter one's sanctuary, close the doors, and henceforth speak only to those who happen to be heirs of the same tradition? In short, is further reflection a private affair? Or is it possible to speak from within the experience of a particular tradition while at the same time testing the deliverances of that tradition against what has emerged and continues to emerge from the broader conversation and feedback? Even though many in the larger audience do not share the experience and assumptions that lie at the core of the tradition in question, can the conversation nevertheless continue?

Only, it seems to us, if the central claims of a given tradition—in our case, the Christian one—can be formulated in ways that take into account the results of the broader conversation. The results of that project may not be the whole story; they may not capture everything that those who belong to the tradition deeply feel and earnestly want to say. Still, to be a rational agent is to want to act, insofar as possible, on beliefs that make sense; and that implies making sense to others— ideally, all others!—and not merely to oneself. There is no reason to think that every belief I hold on the basis of my tradition or my experience will be such that I can explain it—much less justify my holding it—to those who belong to other traditions or have experienced the world in ways that may differ from mine. But as a rational agent, I want to know just how far I can go in justifying my beliefs and actions before I conclude that the project of rational justification has run its course and nothing is left but mystery.

The claims of the Christian tradition focus on a particular historical individual, a Jewish rabbi living in Roman-occupied Palestine in the first century of the Common Era. Debates about the "historical Jesus" are endless, multifaceted, and bewilderingly complex. But they all come down, sooner or later, to a single question: was this an ordinary human life that, thanks to the vivid imagination of early witnesses and later interpreters, took on a false aura of religious significance? Or is there a reason to think that, in the case of Jesus, "something happened"—something, that is, of enduring religious importance? More precisely, is there reason to think that the events of Jesus' life and death made the nature and the core dispositions, the ultimate values, of God present to human beings in a way that, perhaps, they had never been before, and in a way that would have decisive consequences for the relationship between that divine reality and human beings?[1] Is there reason, in other words, to accept what might be called *the Christian proposition*, at least in its most general and least controversial form: that the infinite grace and compassion of the ultimate reality itself were present, and *in some sense* continue to be present, in this particular human being?

This question comes into sharpest focus when what is being debated is whether the man known (in English-speaking countries) as Jesus of Nazareth did or did not come back to life and appear to his disciples at some point reasonably close in time (a few weeks if not a few days) to his execution by Roman authorities. The assumption generally underlying these debates is that if Jesus was resurrected (in some fashion or other), it makes sense to accept *some* version of Christian claims for his theological significance; but if the statements alleging his resurrection are really instances of simple error, legendary development, or pious propaganda (or some combination of those), then Jesus is at best a "symbol" of the divine, or a stimulus to religious emotion and reflection.

This assumption seems plausible, but then the question becomes: what is the right way to understand the claim that Jesus was "resurrected"? Does it require the assumption that Jesus rose from the dead in bodily form and continues to exist as an individual, conscious person? Or are there other ways in which the notion of resurrection might—and perhaps ought—to be understood? As we take up this question, shifting from theism in general to the Christian proposition in particular, it is worth repeating the caveat we presented at the end of the preceding chapter and developed further above. We are now compelled by the nature of Christian claims—as we would be in the case of any religion based on a set of inherited beliefs—to make a major transition, shifting our focus from human experience in general to a body of testimony that emerged from a highly particular location in human history. In developing our response to that testimony, and in whatever sense we may end up affirming the significance of Jesus, we cannot claim the same kind or degree of rational justification that we claimed in the case of our metaphysical arguments or our answer to the problem of innocent suffering. But it is important to keep in mind the other side of our conclusion in Chapter 4: the dependence of religious beliefs on tradition-based experiences does not require one to suspend belief or to deny that the particular religious propositions in question may actually be true.

In this phase of our argument, then, there is no getting around the fact that one's sense of what is plausible or implausible, of what might really have happened, is deeply affected by individual experience and by the particular assumptions that one brings to the testimony in question. It is hard to imagine a body of testimony about which people could be more divided than they are about the biblical texts purporting to describe the death and resurrection of Jesus of Nazareth. But it is unnecessary and, given their influence, even dangerous to conclude that no rational discussion of these texts is possible. Still, there is no doubt that readers' responses to the biblical claims will be significantly affected by their own experience and assumptions.

Those who have experienced what they regard as the presence or love of God through their encounter with the New Testament claims about Jesus are likely to be affected in at least two ways. On one hand, and at something of a secondary level, their experience will give them a greater interest in, and openness to, the possible truth of Christian claims than they might otherwise have. But on the other hand, they already inhabit a spiritual space (so to speak) that they may well go on inhabiting even if they come to understand it differently as a result of the kind of reflection we are now undertaking.

Jesus as "risen"

The salient historical fact about Jesus of Nazareth—that is, the salient fact confirmable by historians—is that he was executed, in a particularly gruesome way, by the Roman authorities who ruled his Palestinian homeland. That claim, at least, is rarely disputed. But one of the main reasons, if not indeed the primary reason, Christians have asserted that Jesus stood in a special relation to God has been their acceptance of a further claim that historians as such cannot confirm: that Jesus in some sense "rose" from death and continued to "appear to" his disciples in a series of events that followed his execution. Here is one of the classic (and according to scholars, one of the earliest) statements of this ancient claim, from a letter written by the missionary Paul to the Christian community he had founded in the city of Corinth:

For I handed on to you as of first importance what I in turn had received: that Christ died for our sins in accordance with the scriptures, and that he was buried, and that he was raised on the third day in accordance with the scriptures, and that he appeared to Cephas, then to the twelve. Then he appeared to more than five hundred brothers and sisters at one time, most of whom are still alive, though some have died. Then he appeared to James, then to all the apostles. Last of all, as to one untimely born, he appeared also to me. (1 Corinthians 15:3–8)[2]

What does it mean, precisely, to say that Christ (presumably meaning Jesus of Nazareth) "appeared"? The traditional way of construing this testimony has been that the man Jesus himself returned in bodily form to greet and converse with his disciples.[3] And that does seem the most obvious way of reading Paul's assertions.

The picture becomes more complicated, however, when one turns from this Pauline testimony to consider the totality of the ways in which these events are depicted in the New Testament. Even if we confine ourselves entirely to canonical texts, ignoring the conflicting signals in the extracanonical "gospels,"[4] what exactly can we say about the earliest Christian understandings of the risen Jesus?

In some places, the claim that Jesus is risen seems to mean that he survives in a human form so closely resembling that of an ordinary human being that he can be mistaken for a traveler or a gardener. Elsewhere, in a later part of the chapter from 1 Corinthians quoted above, he is said to exist in a form as radically different from that of an ordinary human being as a mature plant is different from its seed—so radically different that Paul explicitly asserts that this risen form is impossible to describe or imagine. In some places, the form in which Jesus appears is, once again, that of an ordinary human being, but one who is nevertheless so changed in appearance that he is at first unrecognizable to close acquaintances. Elsewhere in the very same documents where these instances of nonrecognition occur (the Gospels of Luke and John), this same risen Jesus is instantly recognized; and in one case (John), his body in its risen form is so similar to what it was at the point of his death that the unhealed wounds of his execution are clearly visible and, it seems, literally palpable.

He eats fish, but he can pass through walls. He first appears on a road between Jerusalem and a small nearby town (Luke); or he first appears in a garden, somewhere near his tomb (Matthew, John); or he isn't said to appear at all, although his future appearance, in Galilee, is promised by "a young man" (Mark). In two accounts, he first appears to the assembled disciples in Jerusalem (Luke, John); in two other accounts, he first appears to them, or *will* do so, in Galilee (Mark, Matthew). In one place he is first seen by Peter (1 Corinthians); in another place, by Mary Magdalene (John); in another, by the two Marys; in still another, by two unnamed disciples who, however, only recognize him "in the breaking of the bread," after which he instantly disappears (Luke).

In short, it is at the very least an exaggeration to claim that the witnesses share a common understanding of the sense in which the man Jesus of Nazareth rose from the dead and appeared to his disciples and to argue that, for that reason, any viable interpretation of the testimony must be governed by that "shared" understanding.

But in any event, whatever the texts may seem to imply, the claim that Jesus appeared to his disciples in person and perhaps even in a transformed version of his earthly body would seem to be incompatible with the theory of divine action we presented in Chapter 3. After all, if the laws of nature can be broken to the extent of permitting someone to rise physically from the dead, what prevents God from breaking them on other occasions where a far less dramatic miracle would save or restore innocent lives, or at least prevent unnecessary suffering?

Or is there a way to interpret the testimony to Jesus' "resurrection" that does *not* require us to suppose that, in this case, the laws of nature were set aside? Our task in this chapter is to explore several different ways in which "the resurrection event" might be affirmed, to assess their plausibility in light of our earlier conclusions, and, finally, to propose a way of understanding the event that will be consistent both with the requirements of the Christian proposition (as formulated above) and with the implications of what we have discovered so far about the nature and limits of divine action.

Suppose we begin with what might be regarded as the most minimalistic possible interpretation of the claim that Jesus somehow survived his execution and afterwards "appeared" to his disciples: that what the disciples really "saw" was the universal and abiding truth of the vision of reality that had been at the center of Jesus' teachings during his life. For understandable reasons, given then current Jewish beliefs in the bodily resurrection of the righteous, the disciples interpreted the ongoing power of Jesus' teaching as evidence of his continuing personal and indeed bodily existence. But on this account, it was not Jesus himself or anything intrinsically connected with him that so profoundly affected his disciples after his death; it was instead the conceptual and moral power of his teaching that God was a benevolent and forgiving "father."

Jesus himself, on this theory, was a kind of religious genius, someone whose spiritual perspicacity, imagination, and immersion in the traditions of Jewish monotheism enabled him to grasp more clearly and state more powerfully than his predecessors the universal truths that were already implicit in those traditions. Again, it was the abiding power of those truths and of his mode of expressing them—in sermons, parables, and symbolic acts that later came to be regarded as miracles—that led his disciples to regard him as still personally present and active in their lives, and that matters to us today—even those of us who can no longer share the ancient Jewish belief in a literal resurrection of the deceased. We might call this a *symbolic* theory of what Jesus' "resurrection" really amounted to.[5]

A second interpretation of the resurrection testimony also falls, like the symbolic theory, very much on the minimalist end of the spectrum. It regards Jesus not just as a teacher of profound truths but also as a moral and spiritual exemplar—someone who impressed his disciples as actually embodying, in the course of his life and above all in the manner of his death, the self-giving love for others that also characterized the UR as he understood and described it. According to this second theory, Jesus was "resurrected" only in the metaphorical sense that he provided a moral and spiritual model that would inspire and influence subsequent generations of his followers. Call this an *exemplary* theory of Jesus' resurrection, because it translates the idea of Jesus' ongoing life into the way he is not only remembered by his followers but serves as an example for them to imitate.

What makes these two interpretations—the symbolic and the exemplary—so radically minimalistic, at least from the standpoint of traditional Christianity, is that neither requires the assumption that what occurred after Jesus' execution was *theologically* significant. That is, neither retains any active role for the UR—any role for the causal agency of God—in bringing about the experiences that led the disciples to perceive Jesus as either a symbol or an example of the values he taught them to attribute to the divine reality itself. As a result, neither of these interpretations conceives what happened after Jesus' death as involving both sides of the relationship between God and human beings; whatever happened, it happened on the human side alone.

It might seem that such minimalistic interpretations should have an edge over any more robust hypotheses. After all, why not regard self-giving or kenotic love as simply an eternal property of God, the source of an always available opportunity for a proper relationship of human beings with the divine? And why not regard the life and death of Jesus as merely an occasion for a certain collection of human communities to recognize that eternal opportunity and to live in the light of it? Why introduce the complicating notion that *God* may have been involved in whatever the events were that brought this recognition about?

For some readers, including many whose experience is shaped by religious traditions other than Christianity, these symbolic and exemplary interpretations are indeed as far as reflection on the figure of Jesus is likely to go. But does a commitment to science, reason, and respect for religious plurality *require* one to stop here? Or can one be motivated by those commitments and still say something more? Are those who sense the presence and power of ultimacy in the Christian testimony justified in affirming some divine role in the experiences that gave rise to the claim that Jesus was "raised"? Or does any affirmation of a more than merely symbolic resurrection entail a break with science and the modern world?

Recall the conclusions reached in our earlier chapters, including our conclusions about divine agency. Chief among those was the hypothesis that God draws human beings into fellowship with God, partly or even chiefly by "luring" them into harmony with divine values. Such luring turned out to involve the mutual participation of divine and human agencies in the act of communication, rather than a one-directional conveyance of information from the divine to human minds. Without such participation, we argued, acts of divine communication would amount to interventions in the natural order and would make it impossible to solve the problem of evil, because then one could not explain why God would fail to intervene in so many cases where doing so would prevent innocent suffering.

On this account of divine action, whatever God did in response to the death of Jesus cannot have been a miraculous breaking of natural laws. But it doesn't follow that God did simply nothing. After all, if Jesus really was connected with divine values in the way these first two interpretations suggest, and if one is indeed among those who experience the lure of divine values in the New Testament depiction of Jesus, it will seem odd—and more than a little arbitrary—to exclude all divine action from what happened to the disciples after Jesus' death.

Consider, then, a third way to interpret Christian claims about Jesus' resurrection, one that involves a role for divine action or for what is traditionally known as the action of the divine Spirit. On this third account, the disciples, after Jesus' death, found themselves participating in a new reality in which their relationship with the UR had been transformed by the divine grace and freedom they had encountered in the teachings, the acts, and indeed the personal presence of Jesus. We will henceforth call this third view the *participatory* theory of Jesus' resurrection.

Paul and the participatory theory

One of the earliest surviving attempts to spell out the significance of Jesus' death and its aftermath is found in a letter from Paul to the Christian community that, within a few decades of Jesus' execution, had formed in Rome. Paul's fullest account of the meaning of Jesus' life and death occurs in the first eight chapters of this letter to "the Romans." An important premise of his account is Paul's belief that

Jesus was "sent" by God as God's righteous "Son," a role for which Paul also uses the term "Christ," translating the Hebrew word *messiah* or *mashiach*, meaning "the anointed one."[6] According to Paul, the righteousness of Jesus has the surprising consequence of making his execution itself count as an expression of God's love:

> ... God proves his love for us in that while we were still sinners Christ died for us. (Romans 5:8)

But why? Why, exactly, does the fact that Jesus was "righteous" mean that his death counts, for Paul, as an expression of divine love? Part of the answer no doubt is that, as mentioned above, Paul thinks of Christ as having been in some sense "sent" by God for this purpose:

> For God has done what the law, weakened by the flesh, could not do: by sending his own Son in the likeness of sinful flesh, and to deal with sin, he condemned sin in the flesh, so that the just requirement of the law might be fulfilled in us, who walk not according to the flesh but according to the Spirit. (8:3–4)

What mainly makes this divine action effective, however, is not the fact that Jesus was "sent" but that he was righteous (and, for that reason, God's "Son"). Because of Jesus' righteousness, which Paul identifies with Jesus' obedience to God, Jesus overcomes the alienation between divine and human realities that, according to then-current interpretations of the opening chapters of the Book of Genesis, was caused by the disobedience of the first man (Adam):

> Therefore just as one man's trespass led to condemnation for all, so one man's act of righteousness leads to justification and life for all. For just as by the one man's disobedience the many were made sinners, so by the one man's obedience the many will be made righteous. (5:18)

Jesus' righteousness is available to others insofar as their participation in this enactment of divine love enables them to walk "according to the Spirit":

> ... [Y]ou are not in the flesh; you are in the Spirit, since the Spirit of God dwells in you. Anyone who does not have the Spirit of Christ does not belong to him. But if Christ is in you, though the body is dead because of sin, the Spirit is life because of righteousness. (8:9–10)

The NRSV editors note here how freely Paul interchanges the terms "Spirit," "Spirit of God," "Spirit of Christ," and "Christ." Despite his insistence elsewhere on the literal reality of Jesus' resurrection, it is almost as if Paul, in passages like this one, conceives of the risen Christ not so much as an individual person but as the continuation (and availability to believers) of that person's life-giving righteousness— that is, of the life-giving righteousness that Jesus had manifested during his life.

Does Paul also think of the individual man Jesus as literally continuing to exist? No doubt he does; in one passage, for instance, he depicts "Christ Jesus" as seated on a heavenly throne, where he continues his work of reconciling divine and human realities by constantly interceding with God on our behalf:

> What then are we to say about these things? If God is for us, who is against us? He who did not withhold his own Son, but gave him up for all of us, will he not with him also give us everything else? Who will bring any charge against God's elect? It is God who justifies. Who is to condemn? It is Christ Jesus, who died, yes, who was raised, who is at the right hand of God, who indeed intercedes for us. (8:31–4)

Yet it is also "the Spirit" who intercedes for us, and who does so not from a throne next to God but through the medium of our own "sighs too deep for words" (8:26–7). Is that intercessor different from the risen and exalted Christ, or another way of depicting the same reality, to which we have been granted access through the righteousness (= sonship) of Jesus?

There is no way to disentangle Paul's thought in Romans from his engagement with certain late Israelite concepts of law and justification that we can no longer embrace in quite the same way Paul embraced them. Nor are we confident of being able to reconstruct the precise ways in which Paul envisioned the connection between the juridical standing of human beings before God, the concept of divine sonship, and his own experience of fellowship with the community of those united by "the Spirit." Still, what remains intriguing about Paul's account is the possibility it presents of distinguishing between two issues: on one hand, the question of the religious significance of the risen Christ and, on the other hand, the question of whether the man Jesus of Nazareth continued to exist (or resumed existence) after his execution and, if he did, in which of the many possible senses one should understand this "resurrection." While it may well be the case that Paul himself takes such ongoing personal existence for granted, his focus here is not on that but on the continuing effects of Jesus' death as a world-changing expression of righteousness that somehow blends the obedience of Jesus with the loving gift of God.

Somehow—but how, exactly? Is there any way to state such a claim that will make it plausible when judged against the standards for knowledge of our day? Suppose for the moment that Paul's claim here is true, that is, that Jesus' self-surrender to God was at the same time a gift from God; how might this best be understood? Whatever else one might want to say, it's at least clear that, for Paul, Jesus' death and resurrection established a new mode of divine–human relationship. From that point onward, Paul affirms, entering into a relationship with the divine reality has meant participating, somehow, in Jesus' relationship with that reality. (At least this is the case, he writes, for those who find themselves belonging to the tradition in which the witness to Jesus' life and to the meaning of his death has been preserved.) In that sense, Jesus' special relationship with God goes on, and affirmation of the risen presence of Jesus becomes central to the Christian tradition.

Assessing the proposal

This, we suggest, is one way of understanding what it really means, for Paul, to have the "Spirit of Christ": not that Jesus as conscious agent possesses our minds, but that we give ourselves to God by participating in Jesus' self-surrendering obedience to God. In that sense the human relationship with God—again, at least for those who experience themselves as being "in Christ"—has been genuinely transformed by, and continues, the reality of Jesus' individual life and death.

What the life and death of Jesus accomplished, then, on this participatory account was the creation of a new possibility of interaction between God and human beings. Human beings share the "Spirit of Christ" insofar as they enter into the same relationship with God that was embodied in Jesus' self-surrender to the one he called his "Father." The heart of this theory, in other words, is that, *in the event that came to be known as Jesus' resurrection, his self-surrendering engagement with God became newly available, through the agency of the divine Spirit, to his followers, then and since, as the form, model, and condition of their own engagement with the divine.* The event of Jesus' self-surrender somehow became central to "the mutual participation of divine and human agency" that we introduced in Chapter 3 and described in more detail above. Through this event, the disciples saw themselves not only as experiencing a new human insight into the nature of God, but also, somehow, as participating in God through their role as Jesus' disciples. (In itself, this theory is silent on the question of what happened to the individual man Jesus of Nazareth following his execution, although we will return to that question in the next chapter.)

Shifting the focus in this way from Jesus himself to the new relationship with God that his disciples enjoyed has the benefit of shedding light on some of the ambiguities, noted earlier, in the New Testament depiction of the risen Jesus, such as the difficulty that certain disciples have in recognizing him (Luke 24:15; John 20:14) and the way his body is said to retain the marks of his execution (Luke 24:39; John 20:20, 27).[7] If the focus of interest was Jesus' restoration to his former healthy existence—but now in a glorified and immortal body—then it is unclear why these texts would go out of their way, as they seem to do, to emphasize the retention of Jesus' wounds, rather than depicting them as having been healed along with all the other ills his flesh was heir to. In other words, *they seem to focus on Jesus' final act of self-giving, rather than on his new, transformed existence.* Similarly, what is celebrated in Christian worship is arguably not the ongoing life of a man once dead, or even of a God–man once dead, but instead the series of events in and through which the death of Jesus constituted the offer to human beings of a new participation in divine "righteousness."

Again, consider the help the participatory theory offers in making sense of the Pauline interchangeability of terms like "Christ," "Spirit of Christ," and "Spirit" and "Spirit of God," as well as the Johannine notion that Jesus goes away so that the Spirit, that is, "the Comforter" (or Advocate or Helper, as the term *parakletos* is variously translated) can appear in his place (John 16:7). These all become ways of naming the new relationship that is constituted by the coming together of divine compassion and human obedience in the events through which the name of Jesus was exalted to the status of "Son" or "Messiah."

Further, viewing Jesus' resurrection as a transformation of the divine–human relationship, rather than in the first place as something that happens to the man Jesus himself, has the advantage of freeing the significance of Jesus from the vagaries of scholarly debates about the historical accuracy of the New Testament narratives—one of the main

sources of doubt we explored in Chapter 1.[8] It is no longer of primary
importance, on this theory, whether or to what extent the various
conflicting accounts of the disciples' visits to the tomb or subsequent
encounters with the risen Jesus may have been shaped by theological
assumptions, apologetic intentions, patriarchal ideology, or creative
"rescripturings" of the Hebrew Bible.[9] It does not follow that history
or historical scholarship should simply be left behind. It continues to
matter whether or not there existed a person whose life and death
really were such that they brought about a new kind of divine–human
relationship. And it continues to matter whether the disciples who
experienced the abiding possibility and power of that relationship were
or were not deluded. Yet there is no need, on this theory, to reopen
the entire question of Jesus' significance with each new entry into the
scholarly record.

One additional benefit seems worth mentioning: this way of explaining the ancient testimony to Jesus' resurrection provides at least a
modest degree of help in resolving the perennial conflict between
universalist and exclusivist tendencies in Christian thought concerning
the meaning and status of other religions. If the life and death of Jesus
affected the relationship between human beings and God in the ways
this explanation proposes, and if that effect essentially involved the
kind of self-emptying or "kenotic" love and service depicted in the
New Testament accounts of Jesus, then it would seem reasonable to
locate the Spirit of Christ *wherever* such behavior was exhibited or
encouraged. That would support Karl Rahner's answer to the problem
of religious plurality that we addressed in the previous chapter.[10] And
it would at least begin to explain how embracing the scandal of
particularity that lies at the heart of the Christian proposition can
coincide with respect for, and openness to, the particular claims of
other religious traditions.

6

The scandal of particularity, Part II

Jesus and the ultimate reality

The question of uniqueness

In the preceding chapters we acknowledged the difficulties that immediately arise when one moves from general philosophical questions ("Does God exist?") to the highly specific claims of a given religious tradition. Turning in Chapter 5 to one of the most important and distinctive claims of the Christian tradition in particular—the claim that Jesus of Nazareth rose from the dead—we discovered that many Christian accounts fail to grapple with the deep challenges raised by the resurrection testimonies, while some are outright inconsistent. We then used the unresolved difficulties as the basis for constructing what we believe is a consistent and plausible account of the New Testament reports of Jesus' resurrection.

It seemed natural to label that explanation the "participatory theory," because it emphasized the way Jesus' disciples found themselves newly able to participate in the relationship with the ultimate reality (UR) that Jesus himself had enjoyed. Here, once again, is the way we summarized that theory toward the end of the chapter:

The heart of this theory . . . is that, *in the event that came to be known as Jesus' resurrection, his self-surrendering engagement with God became newly available, through the agency of the divine Spirit, to his followers, then and since, as the form, model, and condition of their own engagement with the divine.* The event of Jesus' self-surrender somehow became central to "the mutual participation of divine and human agency" that we introduced in Chapter 3. . . . Through this event, the disciples saw themselves not only as experiencing a new human insight into the nature of God, but also, somehow, as participating in God through their role as Jesus' disciples.

Whatever else it may do, this explanation shifts the primary focus of interpretation from what happened to Jesus immediately after his death to the new relationship between human beings and God that Jesus' death, as the culminating act of his obedience to God, brought about. In revising the traditional emphasis in this fashion, however, it preserves the core Christian assertion that *something really happened*: that there was a genuine development of the divine–human relationship and not merely, for instance, a discovery or reinforcement of an eternal truth about the nature and intentions of God. On this hypothesis, Jesus' disciples, under the influence of their memory of his words and actions and with the guidance of the divine "lure" itself, found themselves able to participate in the same relationship of self-giving obedience to God—an obedience answering and indeed partaking of God's own self-giving love—that they had witnessed in the case of Jesus himself.

Of course it is possible to reject such an account in favor of one of the more minimalistic interpretations we considered at the opening of Chapter 5, but it is unclear why someone who experiences the spiritual power of Christian claims would feel *compelled* do so. In that sense, the participatory hypothesis exemplifies the approach that has characterized the argument of this book from the start: it takes into account the ambiguities and conceptual difficulties affecting certain traditional Christian claims, but it does not shy away from claims about ultimacy that seem both credible and warranted.

It would be easy enough simply to adopt the participatory theory as developed so far and move on. Such an account, after all, would seem to do justice to the central Christian proposition, at least in the very general and minimally controversial form in which we have presented it: that the infinite grace and compassion of the ultimate reality itself were present, and (in some sense) continue to be present, in this particular human being.

But there is a stronger version of the Christian proposition that the participatory theory does not yet explain or justify: the claim that the grace and compassion of God not only were (and in some sense still are) present in this person but were and remain *uniquely* present in him. According to this claim, the Spirit does not merely invite the disciples and their followers to participate in Jesus' relationship with God; the Spirit itself takes on what might be called a Jesuanic form, and what Paul calls the "mind of Christ Jesus" (Philippians 2:5) becomes not only part of what the Spirit conveys to human minds but its definitive and unsurpassable content. Jesus himself, on this account, becomes not only an important instance of human participation in the divine reality but the highest, fullest, most authoritative, or most perfect instance.

There are some rather strong reasons to conclude that this is the interpretation intended in the New Testament texts and the major creeds of the Christian tradition. Not surprisingly, then, many Christian thinkers insist that the strong uniqueness claims are indispensable; to omit them is to silence the astonishing and distinctive "good news" that was the *raison d'être* of the Christian tradition in the first place. Others argue with equal vehemence that the weaker claims canvassed in the previous chapter are sufficient—or indeed more than sufficient—and that, in any event, traditional assertions of Jesus' uniqueness are no longer credible. (Bishop John Shelby Spong is one of the best-known advocates of this latter view, but in fact a wide variety of scholars and theologians take a similar position.)

As this dispute plays out today both in the academy and in the public square, authors seem to divide into two distinct groups: those who will not consider any solution that does not retain the strongest claims about Jesus' uniqueness and divinity, and those who argue that we must resist all such claims. As they face off against each other, opponents in this public (and often strident) debate frequently claim that there *are* no mediating positions, and some maintain that even the effort to seek one is wrong. Perhaps no debate divides contemporary Christians more deeply than this one.

From the opening pages we have argued that such a stark choice is unnecessary. There are many who are attracted to Christian claims regarding the unique significance of Jesus, even deeply committed to them, and yet are given pause by the various reasons for doubt we canvassed in our first chapter. Like the present authors, they find the either/or challenge—the demand either to accept the biblical narratives at face value or to abandon distinctively Christian claims altogether—unhelpful.

In this second chapter on the scandal of Christian particularity, then, we engage in what we hope will be a more nuanced inquiry, asking whether there are ways to conceive the uniqueness of Jesus that avoid some of the problems of traditional accounts and yet nonetheless remain consistent with what we regard as the core commitments of

Christian faith. There will be those whose assumptions rule out this project in advance; where this occurs, we respectfully acknowledge the parting of the ways. All others we encourage to evaluate the arguments. If our conclusions and core arguments fall short, it may be possible to develop responses to the challenges we have identified that are stronger than the one we defend here.

The resurrection appearances

The claim of Jesus' uniqueness—that is, the claim that he should be accorded a status unmatched by any other major religious figure—has often been based on some striking features of the New Testament accounts that we have not yet examined. These texts seem to suggest that what was made present to the disciples in the so-called "resurrection appearances" was not just the significance of Jesus' relationship with God but Jesus "himself." The New Testament documents make the repeated claim that, after his death, Jesus met with his disciples *in person*, in a series of encounters traditionally known to scholars as the resurrection appearances. Each of Jesus' post-mortem appearances reportedly involved a strong impression that the witnesses were encountering the concrete person Jesus as they had known him during his earthly life. At the same time, the appearances themselves were rather few in number and, according to Paul's claim in the passage from 1 Corinthians quoted in Chapter 5, occurred over a finite period and then ceased.

If one wishes to take the New Testament data seriously, one is compelled to ask why, if the participatory theory is sufficient, the New Testament reports draw such a sharp distinction between the original appearances of the resurrected Jesus and later experiences of "the Spirit of Christ." And why did the appearances continue for a finite period and then abruptly stop? (Recall that Paul claims, quite explicitly, that the appearance to him was the last to occur.)

The traditional answer, already present in the texts, would be that Jesus ceased to appear to the disciples in a recognizably personal and indeed bodily form because he was somehow directly transported into the divine reality (this is the so-called ascension of Jesus reported in Acts 1:9–11). On this account, Jesus' personal appearances ceased to occur when his physical body "ascended." From that point on he could only be present to believers through the Spirit. But a belief in the literal ascension of Jesus' physical body from the surface of the earth up through the atmosphere and finally into heaven is not available to those who agree with us that science and the problem of evil conflict with the assertion of physical miracles.

Consider, then, an alternative that might preserve the personal concreteness of Jesus' appearances to his disciples without positing a miraculous resuscitation of his physical body. For some believers, it may seem more plausible to suppose that the mode of presence of the "risen" Jesus would not necessarily have been mediated through his earthly body, and therefore would not have required a divine decision to suspend the natural laws governing events in the physical universe.

Various options are open to those who accept this hypothesis, which we might call *the personal but nonphysical theory of Jesus' post-mortem presence*. There can be no talk of proof here, but there may be ways of showing that, at least in principle, a real albeit nonphysical presence of a person after death is compatible with the presumption against miracles to which the problem of evil led us in Chapter 3.

One set of approaches involves postulating that the early disciples must have experienced a certain kind of event that no longer occurs today. Advocates of this view seek to do justice to the indications in the New Testament texts that, even if Jesus remained somehow present, the nature of his presence changed radically after the finite series of events that occurred soon after his death. They reason that *something* must have been different in the days or weeks after Jesus' death, even if what occurred did not involve the resuscitation (even in some significantly transformed condition) of a physical body.

Suppose, for example, that what happened after Jesus' death was not a case of God's performing some particular action within the created universe but was an altogether different kind of event. Theologians have often viewed the resurrection as inaugurating a new period or epoch in cosmic history. The German theologians Rudolf Bultmann and Wolfhart Pannenberg, among many others, have argued that the end of history somehow became present in the midst of human history.[1]

It is widely acknowledged that "boundary events," such as the creation of the universe and its final apocalyptic end (if there is one), would not obey the same laws as events within the flow of history.

Could the resurrection be thought of in this way? Perhaps it could, if one conceived it as a point at which two different "epochs" overlapped, a point at which two orders or levels of reality intersected, and hence as a unique point of intersection and transition.

In other words, suppose the resurrection is conceived as an onto-logical breakthrough—a radical change in the nature of being itself—accomplished by an unprecedented alignment of human obedience and divine love.[2] If an intersection of epochs took place in this way, for instance through an inbreaking of the final reality (or, in tradi-tional terminology, the *eschaton*) into the midst of history, then events might occur that would be without analogy elsewhere in history—events that witnesses might describe as "a new creation" (2 Corinthi-ans 5:17) or "the kingdom of God" (cf. Matthew 6:33). Perhaps God, in such a moment, would be able to communicate or to act with a clarity, power, or directness not possible at earlier or later points in history. While it lasted, the intersection might involve the ability of human beings in this world to perceive realities in the world beyond—including, perhaps, the reality of Jesus in his final eschato-logical state. One might be able to follow the effects from that point of intersection outwards, like the ripples expanding across a pond after the impact of a falling object. But (on this hypothesis) one would never be able to reconstruct exactly what occurred at the point of intersection itself.

This hypothesis may look like a case of explaining one mystery by a greater one. After all, we have (and indeed *could* have) no more evidence that two different cosmic epochs overlapped or intersected at the time of Jesus' death than we do that his body was physically resuscitated and then later transported to a world beyond this one. But if such an event did occur, it could well have been accompanied by effects that would be inconceivable, even impossible, before or afterwards. In that sense, it would not beg the question of why a benevolent God did not act in a similar way on other occasions, even though doing so might have revealed important truths or pre-vented innocent suffering; such a "kairos" moment (Paul Tillich) would be, by definition, unique.

Still, this hypothesis of a "boundary event" occurring within the flow of history, though possible, will strike some as too far-fetched, or at least too arbitrary, to entertain seriously. Are there other ways, then, of explaining the New Testament testimony—including the testimony that Jesus appeared to his disciples for a finite period and then ceased appearing to them—without engaging in speculations about intersecting worlds or the presence of the final eschatological future in the midst of history?[3] And does one really want to draw such a sharp distinction between the faith of the first disciples and the faith of present-day believers? Those who share these concerns will find themselves drawn to other approaches.

There is one obvious way in which the experience of the earliest disciples differed from that of subsequent believers: they knew Jesus himself face to face, knew him, in fact, extremely well, living with him in the kind of day-to-day intimacy that would inevitably characterize a band of itinerant missionaries dependent on the generosity of those they visited and lacking, among other things, the convenience of modern motels! Suppose the hypothesis of a personal but nonphysical presence is correct; suppose they experienced, after his death, a new encounter with the personality of their deceased rabbi. Is it surprising that, given their preexisting religious expectations of an eventual bodily resurrection of the just, they should interpret that experience as indicating that Jesus himself must have appeared to them not just in personal but indeed in bodily form?

Some have gone as far as to attempt a reconstruction of the psychological process by which the disciples of a charismatic teacher like Jesus might have experienced him as physically present among them.[4] It is not hard to see how such an account might unfold, or how it might be combined with the idea that Jesus was personally but not physically present to his disciples after the crucifixion. After the death of an extremely close friend or relative, we know, many people have the sense that the deceased is still present. Among the effects of grief sometimes reported are visual and auditory experiences.[5] What would happen if such natural psychological phenomena were to coincide with the Spirit's activity in conveying, to the minds of the disciples, the living personal presence of the risen Jesus, whom they had known so intimately?

Perhaps, then, the psychology of grief played a role in convincing the earliest disciples that they had encountered the risen Jesus not only in a personal but in a physical form. Or perhaps their preexisting belief in a bodily resurrection of the just (which they inherited from the Jewish apocalyptic tradition) led them to interpret Jesus' personal presence among them in physical terms. On either of these explanations, the New Testament accounts can be seen as recording experiences by the disciples of the actual presence of Jesus that would not require a breach of physical laws.

Over time, the intensity of these experiences would have faded. Later disciples, who did not know Jesus personally, would describe the ongoing divine experiences of the church as encounters with "the Spirit of Christ" (John, Paul). Perhaps the story of Jesus' bodily ascension into the heavens (Acts 1) began to be circulated some decades after Jesus' death as a way to account for the fact that the initial intensity of the disciples' experience of Jesus' personal presence had diminished in the months following his death.

It appears, then, that the theory we have just now been exploring can provide a reasonably coherent explanation of the New Testament account of what the disciples experienced in the events that scholars call "the resurrection appearances." We have called it the theory of Jesus' personal but nonphysical presence, to distinguish it both from a theory of bodily or physical presence and from the participatory theory developed in the previous chapter. Nor is there any reason to suppose that the risen Jesus, if he existed in this nonphysical form, would have ceased to be present to the disciples' own disciples, or indeed to the many generations of believers who have followed them, even if it was easier for those who had known him personally during his earthly life to recognize his presence. Indeed, if this theory is true, it's possible that the experiences many Christians claim to have may actually be experiences of the presence of the risen Jesus himself in a personal albeit nonphysical form.[6]

But *is* it true? Or, to put this differently, do we have more reason to think that it is true than the competing theories? On some Christian accounts, Jesus himself is personally present in (and perhaps *as*) the Spirit, whenever and wherever the Spirit of God is experienced as revealing Jesus' divine authority and significance. Many will feel that this sense of the continuing *personal* presence of Jesus is the single most important affirmation of, and support for, their faith. One hesitates to raise critical reservations about what is for so many such a fundamental belief. And yet the very importance of this claim also means that it deserves our closest scrutiny. Is the assertion of Jesus' ongoing *personal* presence, even if in a nonphysical mode, plausible?

Personal presence

When turning to a critical examination of some proposition, one tries to reconstruct exactly what is being claimed. In the case of claims for Jesus' continuing personal presence, one needs to ask: what does it mean to say that an individual human being, whose cognitive powers and attention one would expect to be less than infinite, can interact with and be personally present to millions of people over hundreds and hundreds of years? Clearly a person who can hear and respond to the prayers of millions of people at the same time is a different kind of being altogether from the finite subjects we encounter in the world.

The Christian tradition responded to this problem by developing a "two natures" christology—that is, the theory that Jesus was simultaneously human and divine—and, later, by constructing a full theology of the Trinitarian nature of God. Jesus, on the traditional account, was "of one substance with the Father" (*consubstantialem Patri*), as the Nicene Creed puts it. He was thus *Deum verum de Deo vero*, "true God of true God." While he was "in the flesh," either his divine powers were limited or he chose not to exercise them. Perhaps he relinquished being all-powerful and all-knowing while he was a man, or perhaps he *had* unlimited power and knowledge but chose not to avail himself of them, as the nineteenth-century "kenotic" theologians claimed. At any rate, the tradition affirmed, after his death the limitations of his existence as a human individual were removed, and his full divinity became manifest. Yet somehow, even in his eternal state as the second person of the Trinity, he can still be personally available to his followers as the individual person Jesus.

There are many who will affirm that precisely such a transition from finite person to infinite person took place, perhaps because this is what their theological or ecclesial tradition affirms, or because their own experience, like that of countless believers before them, seems to them to suggest that Jesus personally engages and accompanies them. According to what became the dominant tradition of Christian reflection on these matters, the only way to make sense of the resurrection testimony is to suppose that, after his death, Jesus resumed his divine status as the Second Person of the Godhead, so that his very subjectivity was once again constituted by the eternal Logos, the unchanging

Word of God. This implied that the one who entered human history as a Galilean peasant was in some sense *the same individual* as the eternally preexisting Logos. These are extremely difficult claims to interpret, and many in the history of Christianity have treated them as sheer mysteries to be affirmed rather than understood.

For others, however, these complicated theological claims don't quite rise to the level of enduring belief (even though these same persons may continue to use such language in the context of Christian liturgy or worship). These Christian believers may accept the possibility that the man Jesus turned out, after his death, to have been all along identical with an eternal aspect of God, so that he could henceforth be personally present to everyone who "calls upon his name." But they perceive a large gap between possible and likely. Such persons don't think the reasons are actually strong enough to raise this possibility to the status of something they can actually believe. Others are unsure, sometimes affirming the traditional Trinitarian account that makes it possible to speak of Jesus' continuing personal presence and at other times finding themselves not quite able to do so.

And there are other alternatives as well. Although the matter is often presented as if all genuine Christians have actually affirmed the same set of beliefs through the centuries, in fact the major positions have evolved continuously, with influential theologians affirming significantly different interpretations of the creedal formulations or (more often than some want to admit) positions that diverged from one of the creeds in important respects.[7] Consequently, it is not accurate to say that the actual debate is limited to the options of either believing or disbelieving "the traditional account."

Some, of course, will insist that Christianity is an either/or affair: either one affirms without reservation the preexistent Logos or Word of God *and* the full or "hypostatic" union of human and divine natures in Jesus Christ, or one places oneself outside the tradition as a whole. The actual history of Christian thought and belief in fact offers a rather broader and more subtle range of options, however.[8] Without insisting that the traditional accounts are necessarily mistaken or indefensible, one can nevertheless have reason to formulate the core affirmation—what we have identified as the "Christian proposition"—in other ways than the affirmation that Jesus was from birth "one person, two natures." As has happened across the history of Christian reflection, one can adjust the strength of what one affirms in carefully nuanced ways. (Recall that this was one of the two varieties of minimalism that we identified in Chapter 1.) In what follows we explore several of these other responses.

We begin with a variation on the traditional Trinitarian approach, one that does not include the claim that the same person who became the man Jesus already existed in divine form before Jesus was born. This view involves instead the hypothesis that, after Jesus' death, God somehow took this individual's subjectivity into the divine subjectivity, comingling them in such a way that they came to dwell within each other and even to become identical to each other (even if the nature of the resulting identity exceeds human understanding). By using the traditional language of "mutual indwelling" and "co-mingling," we implicitly deny the dichotomy that *either* Jesus continues as the identical person within the godhead *or* Jesus is a merely human model for others to emulate.

On the view we are now considering, Jesus continues to exist as the same person after his death, but he also becomes "true God of true God"; and he is subsequently personally present as the God–man Jesus Christ to all who call upon his name. In the technical jargon of theology, this theory might be classed as a version of the so-called adoptionist heresy—so named because, in contrast to the more ortho- dox theory summarized earlier, it sees Jesus as initially human and only later lifted by God into a status and condition of full divinity. In any event, this adoptionist version of Trinitarian theology may be attrac- tive to those contemporary Christians who can't quite believe (even if they have no way of definitively denying) the complicated assertions of classical Trinitarian thought, but who nevertheless find themselves believing in Jesus' continuing personal presence.

For others, this adoptionist–Trinitarian view will still not be mini- malist enough. Some will not believe, or will only sometimes find themselves believing, the claim that Jesus continued to be *personally* present to his disciples and to subsequent believers as a divine–human agent. Their reluctance to affirm this view is understandable, because serious conceptual issues do indeed arise when one attempts to con- ceive how a single individual can be both infinite and finite at the same time.[9] Is there another position, slightly more minimalist in its claims, that in most other respects stands close to the adoptionist–Trinitarian position we have just considered? And if so, is this view still consistent with what we have been calling the Christian proposition?

We suggest that the participatory theory developed in the previous chapter offers a plausible way of meeting this standard while avoiding the difficulties faced by some of the traditional defenses of Trinitarian language. (We will have occasion to return in a moment to the adoptionist–Trinitarian view that we have just considered.) Recall the core affirmation of the Christian proposition in its strong form: that Jesus of Nazareth uniquely embodied, and in some sense continues to embody, the infinite grace and compassion of the ultimate reality itself. If this claim is true, what becomes available to the disciples after Jesus' death is not just a new relationship with some abstract version of a divine reality but a new encounter with the source of infinite grace and compassion. We discovered, however, at the end of Chapter 3 that the grace and compassion of God can only be defended adequately if it makes sense to suppose that there is hope for a continuation of human existence beyond the grave. Otherwise, the unmerited suffering and despair that have defined the lives of so many human beings over so many millennia seem to be not only pointless but unredeemed and unredeemable. Given that consequence, how can we embrace an explanation of the testimony regarding the resurrection of Jesus that is simply silent about what happens to human beings—because it is silent about what happens to Jesus himself—after death?

It seems clear, then, that a Christian hope for life after death—and therefore Christian theism as we understand it, even in its most minimalistic form—is fully coherent only if it also makes sense to suppose that the personal reality of Jesus did not simply come to an end on a Roman gibbet. Hence an adequate theory of the resurrection testimony cannot entail a denial that Jesus shares the eschatological future available to other human beings. But it *can* stop short of endorsing the belief that Jesus was present to his first disciples after his death as a personal agent, a center of subjectivity with human memories, thoughts, and wishes. The "hope of the resurrection," it turns out, requires a continuing existence after death, for Jesus no less than for others. But, perhaps surprisingly, it does not require that Jesus continue to *appear* as a person to his disciples, ancient or modern, on this side of the divide.

That last observation raises a final question about the theory that the Spirit of God made and makes Jesus literally and personally present to his disciples, albeit in a nonphysical form. If the Spirit was able to do this in the case of Jesus, why would the Spirit refrain from making other persons personally even if nonphysically present to those left behind in this world? After all, there are countless cases in which people are profoundly saddened and bewildered by the death of a loved one; countless cases in which they would be consoled and inspired by a perception of their loved one's ongoing presence. Just as we could not explain, in Chapter 3, why God would prevent one case of innocent suffering while permitting others, one is hard pressed here to explain why God would favor one group of mourners with a consolation denied to others.[10]

In this section we have been forced to confront some of the most difficult conceptual (and even moral) challenges to the theory that Jesus was and is personally present to his followers. The difficulties in conceiving how a finite person could be identical to an infinite and omnipresent divine Spirit highlight, once again, the comparative strength of the participatory approach we developed in Chapter 5. According to the participatory theory, it is not Jesus himself who is literally made present—either in bodily or in continuing personal form—to the minds of his followers. What is made present instead is a new relationship with the divine reality in which Jesus' followers find themselves able to participate. What they encounter is the Spirit of Christ, who calls them to the same kenotic or self-giving love that Jesus embodied and enacted in his relationship with the one he called "Father."

How, then, does the participatory theory explain the New Testament data we noted earlier: namely, the strongly personal character, finite number, and eventual cessation of the "appearances" of Jesus? This is a problem, in fact, that the participatory theory shares with the theory of Jesus' ongoing personal (but nonphysical) presence. Both face the challenge of explaining why at least some of the earliest disciples would have claimed (as reported in the biblical texts) that they had encountered the risen Jesus "in person" and even "in the flesh" and that this experience came to an end after a certain period of time.

As we saw earlier, there are various possible ways of imagining what might have occurred. Consider, for instance, a variation on a hypothesis we briefly explored earlier: the disciples' vivid memory of Jesus, combined with the strong apocalyptic emphasis in their religious tradition, predisposed them to interpret their Spirit-led discovery of Jesus' theological significance as a sign of actual bodily resurrection. From that point of view, it would not be surprising that experiences of personal encounters would be reported by the earliest disciples, while their later followers—Paul, for instance, and the author of the Fourth Gospel—would increasingly focus instead on the community's experience of encountering the "Spirit of Christ." Or, as also noted earlier, there remains the possibility—compatible both with the participatory theory and with the theory of Jesus' personal presence—that a unique alignment of human and divine wills brought about, at the point of Jesus' death, an intersection of divine and human realities (a moment of "eschatological inbreaking") in which it was temporarily possible to "see" the risen Christ.[11] In any event, it would seem that the participatory theory fares at least as well, in handling the New Testament data, as the theory that Jesus himself was and is somehow present, in person, in what the Spirit presented and still presents to the minds of his followers.

But there is one final question that the participatory theory, in itself, does not and cannot answer: do we have reason to think that Jesus was not only an influential, even world-changing instance of human participation in the divine reality but so complete or perfect an instance of such participation that, after his death, the very nature of divine–human interaction took on a Jesuanic character? Do we have reason, in other words, to accept the strong Christian claim that Jesus' relationship with God was such that, through this single human being, God has communicated with humankind in a uniquely authoritative and unsurpassable way? Or does that claim go beyond what can be rationally assessed, even by those who find themselves located within the gravitational field defined by Christian experience and assumptions—let alone by those who belong to other traditions or who stand outside all of them?

"The Spirit of Christ": A Spirit-centered theory of the resurrection

The purpose of this and the previous chapter has not been to determine once and for all "what really happened" in the days, weeks, and months that followed the death of Jesus, a period in which his disciples were somehow transformed from a bereaved, scattered, and frightened cell into the active core of a robust community and then a movement that quickly swept across the Mediterranean world. The aim instead has been to show how much of, and in what sense, the received accounts of what happened could have been true, without entailing a theory of divine action that would make it difficult if not impossible to explain why God did not act in a similar way on other occasions.

We have considered a number of possibilities, but the account that has emerged so far with the greatest clarity and coherence is the one we have called the participatory theory. Behind the resurrection testimony, this theory suggests, is an experience on the part of the earliest Christians of a new relationship with the ultimate, divine reality. In this new experience of ultimacy they discovered that the self-giving love of Jesus had brought about a new possibility of divine–human relationship in which they were invited to share.

But, as we saw, this account stops short of answering what is arguably the boldest question raised by the Christian tradition: whether the infinite grace and compassion of God were not just present but uniquely, definitively, unsurpassably present in this particular human being. Can we draw on the resources of the participatory theory in developing a possible answer to that question? In particular, can we extend it in a way that may help explain the sense in which Jesus of Nazareth and the events of his life and death may have played a uniquely powerful and authoritative role in the manifestation of divine grace and compassion, rather than serving as one of perhaps many equally significant instances?

At the end of Chapter 2 we defended the notion of an intentional creation of the universe by an ultimate reality that is not less than personal. If such a being intentionally creates a world outside itself, we argued, self-giving love for others could well constitute at least part of the motivation of that act. If love in this sense is already an aspect of God, it must be implicit in *all* interactions between God and creation. The Christian claim, however, in its strong or what might be called its *fully christological* form, is that something was added by the life and death of Jesus that transformed the relationship between God and human beings in an unparalleled and indeed an unsurpassable way.

We have characterized the self-giving love of Jesus—the love in which his disciples and their followers were and are invited to participate—as both responding to and, in some sense, embodying the self-giving love of God. Suppose we now press that idea a step further by proposing that Jesus was not just someone who was generous to others and even willing to endure suffering on their behalf.

Suppose his love for others was so perfect that, for that very reason, it became a revelation of the divine love itself. That could only be the case if perfect love for others was at the same time perfect responsiveness, perfect obedience, to the divine lure and therefore to the divine will. For only in that case would what Jesus *did* amount to a definitive revelation of what God *is*. Or to put this in terms that more fully take into account the logic of *participation*: it is through his perfect responsiveness to God's self-giving love that Jesus simultaneously reveals that love and transforms it into its definitive *human* form.

This, we suggest, is the sense in which one may suppose that Jesus' obedience to God actually made *God's* infinite grace and compassion present to the world. If the christological hypothesis is right, God incorporated what Paul calls the "mind of Christ Jesus" (again, Philippians 2:5) into the divine lure, so that Jesus' obedience to God and love for others became the primary content that the Spirit of God conveys to human minds.

Earlier we referred to the so-called adoptionist christologies. These are versions of Trinitarian thought in which Jesus is regarded not as identical with a preexisting divine being—the eternal Second Person of the divine Trinity—but as exalted to that status during his life or after his death. On this view, God responds to Jesus' perfect obedience by incorporating him into the Godhead and transforming him into a divine participant in the community of God's Triune life. (Of course, this doesn't imply that Jesus' perfect obedience occurred all on its own, without any divine support and assistance. Given the participatory theory of divine action developed in previous chapters, a close partnership of divine and human wills would have been involved from the start.)

Well, suppose something like that notion is actually true. What does this christology look like if developed without the assumption that the finite person Jesus of Nazareth becomes in the process identical with a divine being, so that he is capable (for example) of communicating simultaneously with millions of praying believers?

Suppose what happens is not that the man Jesus acquires a divine capacity for infinite awareness but that God makes the perspective of a finite human being an essential and defining aspect of God's interaction with creation. To put this thought in what is of course a metaphorical form: it isn't that Jesus suddenly becomes capable of looking through the infinite eyes of God, but that God chooses to look through the finite eyes of Jesus. We see God through Jesus' self-giving love, and God sees us through Jesus' self-giving obedience. *Together, these movements of love for the other on the part of both creator and creature constitute the self-emptying or kenotic "mind of Christ,"* and that new reality becomes at the same time the Spirit of Christ in which both humanity and God participate. From that moment on, what the Spirit conveys to Jesus' disciples, to their followers, and perhaps in some fashion to human beings in general is the mind of Christ—more exactly, as Paul writes, the mind of Christ Jesus—both as an essential aspect of God and as a living reality in which they too are now invited to participate.

With this "adoptionist" addition, the relationship between Jesus and the divine Spirit takes on a newly significant and indeed definitive form, and we arrive at what might be called a *pneumatological* (i.e., Spirit-centered) theory of Jesus' resurrection. Jesus himself, on this account, remains a person, like other persons. Only in this way, we believe, does it make sense to say that "in every respect [he] has been tested as we are" (Hebrews 4:5). After his death he is evermore sustained in his unique personhood by his eternal existence within the life of God, a destiny that all his followers may hope to share. At the same time, the "mind of Christ"—the attitude of self-giving love and compassion that Jesus embodied in his earthly life and death—becomes an aspect of the infinite God, the central reality that the Spirit of God thereafter conveys to human beings and that it invites them to share.

This way of characterizing what the Spirit conveys to human minds risks, we realize, a serious misunderstanding. It may sound as if, on this account, what the Spirit conveys is merely a certain pattern of behavior, or merely a new kind of ethical principle, and therefore something finally detachable from the concrete historical reality of Jesus of Nazareth. Although that is certainly one possible way to interpret the resurrection testimony, the participatory theory of divine action supports a different option, one closer to the intent of the view we considered earlier, which holds that Jesus remained personally but not physically present to his disciples after his death. Call this option a Spirit-centered or *pneumatological* version of the participatory theory. On this second and bolder interpretation, what the Spirit conveys is not just the mindset or attitude of Jesus, taken as an ethical or philosophical principle, but the definitive reality and authority of Jesus' self-surrendering obedience to the ultimate reality he knew as "abba," "father," an obedience that is at the same time his self-surrendering openness to the needs of other persons. In that sense, an essential aspect of Jesus himself would continue to be spiritually present to his disciples after his death.

But how, exactly, is what the Spirit makes present essentially connected to Jesus, and not just a religious ideal or ethical principle that is merely *associated with* the memory of Jesus? The answer must include an eschatological dimension: Jesus, after his death, is sustained by God not just as another finite person but as *the* finite subject whose will is most fully and perfectly conformed to the will of God—and for that reason as the "head" of an eschatological community whose members in varying degrees participate in that unity of divine and human will. Readers of the New Testament will recognize here the influence of Jesus' "high priestly prayer" from the Gospel of John. In that account Jesus says that after he goes away he will not return to his disciples as the person they knew before his death. Instead, he will send a "Comforter" or "Consoler" (*paraklētos*), the Holy Spirit. This Spirit will dwell with and be "in" the disciples and will bear witness or "testify" to Jesus; he will "take what is mine and declare it to you" (John 16:14).

What the Spirit testifies to, on this account, is the reality of that actual, concrete eschatological community, in which we also are invited to participate. And in making that community present, the Spirit necessarily makes present the reality of the one whose life and unique relationship with God created that community, defines it, and continues to sustain its growth.

7

Doubt and belief

How do we assess our beliefs?

O ur aim in this book has been to explore a certain account of what is ultimately the case, an account that many continue to find compelling, at least in its general outlines if not in all its traditional details. In the process, we have considered the most powerful reasons for doubting the claims this account entails. Although the objections sometimes required modifications, they also made it possible to develop (what we hope are) more adequate answers. The goal, at any rate, was to develop a position that might be embraced by those who want their most important beliefs to be rational, that is, to be based, as far as possible, on what they have reason to think is actually true.

Implicit in that project has been a certain conception of what it means to be a rational agent, a person who cares about whether she *should* hold the beliefs she is inclined to hold. This is not to suggest that human beings are entirely, or even largely, rational in their approach to their own beliefs. Some will care more than others about whether they possess reasons to believe that others—or even they themselves— should regard as good. But even those who *do* want their beliefs to be based on good reasons will find themselves relying on some beliefs they can't rationally justify. No one—not the greatest philosopher nor the most rigorous scientist—is capable of citing a rational basis for every belief she holds. Nor is there a single standard of rationality to which all one's beliefs might be held. As we will show in a moment, there are varying degrees of rational justification, and the degree of one's justification for holding any particular belief changes over time with the state of debate on the subject in question and with one's relation to the relevant communities of inquiry. In the paragraphs that follow, we will distinguish as many as six different levels or degrees of justification.

That said, our theory of rational agency is, at bottom, a simple one. Its fundamental premise is that what it means to be a rational agent is to want the beliefs on which one relies to be beliefs that, as far as one knows, are likely to be true, and indeed are *more* likely to be true than the alternatives. Unfortunately, however, there is no way to check if one's beliefs are likely to be true by comparing them directly with the reality one hopes they are tracking. The reason is obvious: the results of any checking one might do themselves take the form, necessarily, of beliefs that would have to be checked in turn. So, once again, there is no way of stepping outside one's beliefs to see which ones correspond to the way things really are. The best an agent can do is to make sure, insofar as possible, that her reasons for holding a belief are better than the reasons she might have for rejecting it.

To say that reasons can be better or worse is to imply, however, that there is a basis for comparing them. And since that basis cannot be the direct observation of reality itself, what can it be? Our answer is that, in any given sphere of inquiry, a belief counts as rationally justified if it is held for a reason or reasons that the relevant community of experts (henceforth RCE) either regards as good, or would regard as good if that community had the right amount and kind of information.[1]

In the best case, most RCE members will simply agree that the agent's belief is the right one to hold. If I want to know the date on which a famous person died, I look it up in a well-known encyclopedia, which I have reason to regard as a reliable distillation of expert opinion on the fact in question; the belief I acquire as a result of this procedure is one I regard as fully justified. In cases where there is a clear consensus of expert opinion, it is hard to imagine a belief that I would feel more strongly justified in holding.

But it would be absurd to insist that a belief is only rationally justified if the experts happen to share one's reasons for holding it. After all, even in the case of something as uncontroversial as the date of an important event, I might acquire a reason to conclude that the experts are simply wrong, say because my research has traced their belief back to a clerical error that, once made, was repeated through many generations of later reports (something that, as any historical scholar will tell you, actually occurs with a perhaps surprising frequency). More interestingly, I might have reason to conclude that the experts had been led astray by an ideological bias. The history of science is replete with instances in which a new hypothesis conflicts with received opinion and is therefore mistakenly ruled out of court. (One thinks, for instance, of the long-resisted hypothesis that peptic ulcers were caused by a certain bacterium, *Heliobacter pylori*, a hypothesis that contradicted the RCE's certainty that peptic ulcers were caused by stress.)[2]

In cases like the ones just described, the agent has what we will call a *theory of error* for the RCE's failure to endorse her reasons for belief. This need not be a theory of error in the technical sense in which philosophers use the phrase, which generally requires demonstrating how a set of data is being misinterpreted and why, if it were correctly interpreted, it would necessarily lead to the correct conclusion. Take, for example, the long-held belief that the sun revolves around the earth. Scientists today have a theory of error for that belief that provides the correct explanation and at the same time accounts for why observers were once misled: because the sun does, in fact, appear to move in an arc across the sky. Although matters of religious belief are not quite as clear-cut, one is sometimes able to produce a strong argument for a belief *as well as* to show why the RCE's widespread rejection of the belief is mistaken. In such cases, it would be better from the agent's own point of view if the experts agreed with her, but it would seem absurd to suggest that her belief was rendered irrational by their failure to do so.

Suppose, however, the agent *lacks* a theory of error for the RCE's disagreement with her. Suppose she does not regard the RCE as making some kind of identifiable mistake but instead regards the RCE's attitude as perfectly reasonable, given the RCE's point of view. We might say that, in that case, the agent regards the claim in question as *irreducibly controversial*, a matter about which reasonable people can and do appropriately disagree.

What factors make a claim irreducibly controversial? They may include the dependence of belief in that claim on particular kinds of experience. Imagine, for example, that an agent or group of agents has had specific experiences that are not shared by the RCE. Although religious experiences are the classic example, they are not the only kind of experience that might qualify; nor are experiences the only types of factors that can lead people to hold beliefs the RCE does not have sufficient reason to endorse. I might believe that a particular suspect is guilty of a crime because I sense something strange in his behavior after the crime occurs, even though I do not expect the RCE to view my "evidence" as sufficient. In many cases, decisions on irreducibly controversial topics are extremely complex, relying on the differential assessment of multiple intuitions, assumptions, data, and inferences. Can an agent who holds a belief about a matter *that she herself regards as irreducibly controversial* still be justified in holding the belief in question?

We submit that she can, and that there are degrees of justification in the case of beliefs about irreducibly controversial matters just as in the case of ordinary beliefs that can be confirmed or disconfirmed by "checking the facts." Even if the RCE does not endorse the agent's belief or her reasons for holding it, the RCE may nevertheless agree that the agent's reasons are good reasons *for her*—good reasons, that is, for someone who has had the kinds of experiences the agent has had, or who has other reasons, not universally shared or accessible, that incline her to hold a particular set of beliefs.

Alternatively, the RCE may decide that the agent's reasons for belief are not the kind of reasons one could rationally cite as justifying the belief in question. They may be so vague, complex, or uncertain that the agent herself cannot see any way of subjecting them to public discussion, including even a discussion of whether such reasons might be good reasons for someone in her particular situation. In that case, the agent will have to acknowledge that her justification is weaker than in the previous case—weaker, that is, than it would be if the RCE endorsed her reasons only as reasons *for her*. When this happens, several options may become available to her. She may decide that her belief is no longer one she can hold rationally, even if she finds herself compelled to hold it nonetheless. Or she may shift her attitude altogether from believing to merely *hoping* that what she once believed will still, in the end, turn out to be true. Finally, she may not even hope the belief is true but still regard the proposition in question as a useful metaphor for something she believes and, in that spirit, use it at least occasionally to guide her thoughts and actions.

What we are gradually unfolding here is a typology of degrees of rational justification an agent may regard herself as having for relying on—that is, guiding her thoughts and actions by—a certain claim or proposition. This typology may be easier to follow if we now step back and present it in slightly more formal terms. Let S, then, be the agent or subject whose rational justification is in question; let P be the proposition that is the object of her belief or (to make room for cases like hoping the claim is true) a proposition to which she is in some sense committed. Finally, let us continue to use RCE to stand for the relevant community (or communities) of experts on the topic the proposition concerns. Here, then, is the series of six degrees of justification to which the foregoing remarks have been pointing:

(1) S believes P and believes that P is endorsed by the RCE—or will be so endorsed once the RCE has an opportunity to evaluate S's reasons for believing.

(2) S believes P but does not believe that P is, or expect that P will be, endorsed by the RCE. But S believes the RCE is mistaken; S thinks she knows *why* the RCE is mistaken, and what it would take to correct the error.

The first of these degrees or levels of justification is perhaps self-explanatory. Another way to describe the second level would be to say that, in such cases, S possesses a theory of error, in the sense explained earlier, to account for what she regards as the RCE's mistaken rejection of P.

(3) S believes P but does not expect P to be endorsed by the RCE. But in this case S cannot point out the specific mistake or mistakes that she thinks the RCE is making. S therefore regards P as irreducibly controversial. Yet given her particular experience and point of view, S has what she regards as good reasons to believe P, reasons she thinks the RCE also should regard as good reasons *for an agent in her position*. S, in other words, regards belief in P as rationally indicated, but only for agents who share certain of her assumptions and/or experiences.

These are cases, once again, in which S thinks the RCE should acknowledge that, if one had certain intuitions or experiences, or made certain assumptions that led one to assess the data in a certain way, it would make sense to believe the proposition in question.

But then there are cases in which S herself is unsure how good her reasons are; hence the next level:

(4) S believes P but, as in (3), does not expect P to be endorsed by the RCE, cannot point to a mistake she believes the RCE is making,

and therefore regards P as irreducibly controversial. She still has reasons to believe, but now the inferences are complicated enough, the possible criticisms serious enough, and/or the experiences from which she derives those reasons unclear enough that the status of P seems to S herself to be ambiguous. So she no longer claims that the RCE should regard her reasons as good ones, and she does not regard her belief as rationally indicated, even for an agent with her particular experiences and point of view. Yet S nevertheless has enough reason to believe P that it remains rationally *permissible* for her to do so.

This level of commitment, we will suggest in a moment, can be quite important to religious life. But it is also the most difficult to define or describe or evaluate, because in this case S herself is not certain whether her reasons are good ones, or whether P is something she can fully or constantly believe, even if she sometimes experiences moments of intense conviction that P is actually true. At times, she may find herself unable to continue believing, in which case her attitude will likely shift to the next level:

(5) S is attracted to P and hopes it will turn out to be true. Perhaps she occasionally finds herself believing it, but she does not have what she regards as good reasons to persist in doing so. If she continues to seek confirmation of P and to guide her thoughts and actions by the possibility of its turning out to be true after all, she does so as a "seeker," that is, someone who is not currently a believer (though she perhaps once was) but is attracted to the possibility of someday coming to believe.[3]

The kind of hope that, at this level, takes the place of actual belief can be strong enough to shape a person's entire life and to guide many or even most of her most important decisions. In that sense, it can provide the basis of a religious self-identity that gives rise to the same kinds of religious practices and moral choices one would find in the case of an actual believer. In such cases we might speak of an attitude of *hope-plus-faith*, even when actual belief is lacking or is only intermittently present.

The reasons for one's hopes are generally harder to confirm than the reasons for one's actual beliefs. Yet hope can influence a person's most fundamental values as well as a myriad of day-to-day decisions. The possibilities one glimpses during certain moments of experience may give one reason to hope that a certain proposition is true, to seek confirmation of it, and to guide one's thoughts and actions by the possibility that it will turn out to be true after all. In such cases hope serves as a sort of "cognitive policy" that nonetheless falls short of actual belief. Indeed, in the context of religious life, where the status of many of the central propositions is so unclear (even, sometimes, for the religious person herself), hope-plus-faith may need to play much of the role that actual belief plays in philosophical and scientific contexts.

But what happens when S does not even *hope* that P will turn out to be true, and yet still regards it as in some sense a useful or interesting claim? That question leads to the final level of our typology:

(6) S does not believe P, or perhaps believes that P is actually false if understood literally, and therefore does not even *hope* that P is true. But S does regard P as a valuable metaphor for a proposition or set of propositions she does regard as true. She may at times allow herself to suspend her disbelief in P while participating in religious practices like prayer or worship; she does so, however, with at least a tacit awareness that P is not true in its own terms but is really, for her, a metaphor for something else.

Here we touch on an important but rather subtle aspect of religious life, as well as of other human practices that involve an element of ritual. In certain circumstances, an agent may experience a moment of conviction in which she finds herself believing a proposition that, ordinarily or on reflection, she would not regard as literally true. Such moments are akin to what Samuel Taylor Coleridge famously called "that willing suspension of disbelief for the moment, which constitutes poetic faith," although Coleridge's statement about our experience of poetic fiction suggests a greater degree of deliberateness and perhaps distance than applies to religious moments of what might be called extraordinary or excessive conviction.[4]

Again, such moments are not confined to religion; something similar occurs, for instance, when one attends a secular funeral and finds oneself believing an attribution of virtues to the deceased that, on reflection, would strike one as exaggerated at best. In religious cases, such moments can play an important and even essential role in creating a shared set of experiences that bind together members of an otherwise disparate community and in the spiritual formation of individual believers. In fact, one striking characteristic of adept practitioners is their ability to enter into such moments with great regularity and frequency, all the while preserving a tacit awareness that the claims in question may well not be literally true. (In that sense, it is quite possible to be a minimalist regarding the doctrines in which one fully and literally believes, without being a minimalist when it comes to religious practice and experience.)

We recognize how difficult it is to assess such a personal and urgent matter as one's own religious belief (or disbelief, or inability to believe) in light of these six levels of justification. Many people find it difficult to look so closely and dispassionately at their core convictions, to hold them at arm's distance, as it were, and to admit, even to themselves, where they have good grounds for their religious beliefs and where they do not. Nevertheless, there is something to be said for making sure, insofar as one can, that one's most important decisions are based on reasons one has grounds to think are good ones. There is also a benefit, we would argue, in the humility that comes from discovering that one's reasons, even for beliefs one can't help holding, are not as strong as one would have liked them to be.

Doubt, uncertainty, and Christian belief

There are no doubt other ways of constructing a typology of beliefs and belief-like attitudes, but the levels we have distinguished here would seem to provide a sufficiently nuanced framework for assessing the rational status of belief in the various theses we have presented in this book.

Many of the scientific claims summarized in Chapter 2 would seem to qualify as level-1 claims, that is, claims one would expect to be endorsed by the relevant community of experts, and some of the philosophical arguments used in Chapters 2 and 3 represent standard philosophical moves that might also qualify at this level. But the relevant communities of inquiry are divided on what implications to draw from these level-1 claims, which means that the inferences we have drawn from them will rise, at best, to level 2. (Unfortunately, many scientists and philosophers who write on these questions make rather stronger assertions about the status of their own arguments. Richard Dawkins's widely publicized claims about biology and religion, which he clearly regards as enjoying level-1 status, offer a rather dramatic example of overstated conclusions.)[5]

We suggest, in any event, that belief in the conclusions presented in the first four chapters—conclusions that together constitute our case for minimally personalistic theism (MPT)—should be regarded as having a level-2 status. In other words, these are beliefs that, in our judgment, the RCE ought to endorse, and *would* endorse were it not for the prevalence of certain mistaken assumptions about, for instance, what is or is not compatible with modern science.

That does not mean we regard our conclusions as certain or incorrigible. In one case—our response in Chapter 3 to the "argument from neglect"—we presented a hypothesis that we could only claim was more *plausible* than the alternatives; we could not claim to know that it was actually true. Other conclusions—for instance, that the ultimate reality is a not-less-than-personal being—enjoy strong enough support that it makes sense, in our view, to believe with some confidence that they are actually true. They thus belong on level 2 of the typology above, even if the arguments given on their behalf are more controversial than certain other level-2 claims. Our argument that the UR must share at least some human values, on the other hand (see Chapter 2, note 26), is not primarily a hypothesis at all but a judgment about what human agents must assume if they are to make sense of their own rational agency. Indeed, it functions as a kind of wager: one cannot prove that human rational agency isn't finally based on an illusion. But one puts one's money (as it were) on one's sense that rational agency really is possible, making whatever assumptions that wager entails. It seems necessary to bet on one's own rational agency in this way, even if one can't show that those assumptions are actually true. In any event, despite all the differences in the logical nature and status of these various conclusions, we do claim that the RCE should endorse our reasons for reaching them.

Chapters 5 and 6, however, are another matter, for reasons developed at some length in our discussion of religious plurality in Chapter 4 and mentioned again at the beginning of Chapter 5. As one descends from metaphysics to the concrete and properly controversial claims of actual religious traditions, reasons for belief increasingly involve experiences that generally (although not necessarily) correlate with participation in the traditions themselves. Justification shifts—indeed, declines—to level 3, where the RCE withholds its endorsement and, in so doing, cannot be regarded as making some kind of mistake. But at least in some cases, the RCE *can* be expected to endorse the rationality of holding the belief for those who bring to the claims in question certain kinds of experience or certain assumptions that constitute, for them, good reasons to believe. The agent herself, in such cases, should acknowledge that her reliance on experience and assumptions that others cannot share diminishes her degree of rational justification. But she is justified nonetheless.

Note, however, the proviso: personal and communal experience and assumptions confer justification *at least in some cases*; but not, we suggest, in all. There are some beliefs that an agent will find it impossible to reject, or to which she will at least remain strongly attracted, although she cannot claim reasons for belief that the RCE would regard as good reasons *even for her*. In that case, her level of justification descends from level 3 to level 4, and possibly further, to a level at which the most she can do is *hope* a certain claim is true, or even to the point where she regards the claim in question as a metaphor for something else.

In actual religious life, an agent's sense of where she stands in relation to the claims of the tradition in which she finds herself is likely to slide up and down the scale of justification in response to a host of internal and external factors. A further wrinkle we have not yet mentioned is that belief itself is a matter of degree. It is perfectly possible—indeed, it often occurs—that an agent will adhere more strongly to a belief she regards as only minimally justified, or even as irrational, than to a belief to which she assigns a high degree of rational justification. Thus I may feel utterly justified in my belief that an event occurred when the encyclopedia says it did, but I am not much attached to that belief and would not be much affected if it turned out to be false. I may be far more strongly attached to a belief—say, about the wisdom of a certain course of action—that I know is endorsed at most by a minority of those who have considered it.

How should we apply this complex picture to our tentative conclusions in the previous two chapters about the meaning and the fate of Jesus of Nazareth? We opened the first of those chapters by mentioning ways of understanding the significance of Jesus' alleged resurrection—that he became an abiding symbol or example of divine grace and compassion—that would seem to be uncontroversial to anyone who accepts our earlier conclusions about the nature and dispositions of the ultimate reality (UR), that is, anyone who accepts our minimally personalistic theism (MPT). Although we quickly moved beyond those ways of interpreting the resurrection testimony, taken simply as assertions about Jesus they would seem to have something close to the same status as MPT itself and therefore to reside at level 2.

We then moved on to what we called the "participatory theory" of Jesus' resurrection, proposing that the Jesuanic model of self-surrendering compassion became part of the content of divine communication with Jesus' disciples and their followers, and perhaps of divine communication with subsequent disciples and with human beings in general. Although this theory will not be accepted by all who accept MPT, the relevant communities of experts should have no trouble acknowledging that it is rational for a believer in MPT who experiences the spiritual power of Jesus as remembered in Christian scripture and worship to accept the resurrection in this carefully defined sense. Hence the participatory theory, at least in this initial form, seems to us to warrant an epistemic status of level 3.

In Chapter 6, however, we went beyond the participatory theory—or, more precisely, we explored a stronger and inherently more controversial extension of it. We considered the possibility that Jesus was more than a saint or prophet whose teachings, attitudes, and mode of life were endorsed and made present by the UR in its subsequent communication with human minds. On this stronger theory, which eventually led us to the Spirit-centered or *pneumatological* theory, we wrote,

the Spirit does not merely invite the disciples and their followers to participate in Jesus' relationship with God; the Spirit itself takes on what might be called a Jesuanic form, and what Paul calls the "mind of Christ Jesus" (Philippians 2:5) becomes not only part of what the Spirit conveys to human minds but its definitive and unsurpassable content. Jesus himself, on this account, becomes not only an important instance of human participation in the divine reality but the highest, fullest, most authoritative, or most perfect instance.[6]

Religiously compelling as it may be, however, the Spirit-centered theory of Jesus' resurrection is attended by conceptual and evidential difficulties that give it a lower epistemic status than the participatory theory in its weaker form. It faces the daunting challenge of arguing that any single human being has enjoyed a unique and unsurpassable relationship with God—a relationship amounting, on the strongest or most orthodox versions of the Christian proposition, to actual identity. Even if one stops short of the strongest Trinitarian claims, how might such an argument even begin? One would have to survey all the major religions, and the lives of all the influential prophets, in an attempt to show that God was not as active in their lives as in the life of Jesus. Given the number of candidates and the paucity of evidence, that would be a tall order. But even then one could not be quite certain. What if a relatively unknown saint once lived in a small village, a person who was uniquely open to the lure of God? What if her brief life demonstrated a fusion with the divine will that matched or even exceeded Jesus's model of self-giving, even though the details of her life have mostly been lost to history?

It does not follow from these difficulties that no case can be made for the unique authority of Jesus and of what Jesus "revealed" and therefore of what Christians perceive about the nature and purposes of the UR. But it seems to us that many of the most prominent attempts to make this case have depended on exaggerated claims about what the available evidence can establish. Some have argued, for instance, that there is a possible being that has the property of "maximal excellence" in every possible world (which implies that it has omniscience, omnipotence, and moral perfection in every world), and that the God revealed in Christianity clearly meets this standard.[7] Others have argued that there is objective evidence for the truth of the core Christian claims, whereas there is no objective evidence for the truth of opposing religious claims. For example, numerous Christian authors have attempted to make a positive case for the historicity of Jesus' resurrection, often understood as resulting in objectively observable post-mortem "appearances" of Jesus that could never be explained in naturalistic terms.[8] A different kind of evidential case was offered by C. S. Lewis, who famously argued that there are only four possible understandings of Jesus' identity: liar, lunatic, legend, or Lord. Since the evidence (Lewis claimed) is clearly against the first three possibilities, and there is no fifth option, belief in Jesus' uniquely divine lordship is rationally indicated.[9]

Without pausing to recount all the criticisms that might be (or have been) raised against these apologetic arguments—including those we offered in the previous chapter—we note merely that they remain highly contested. It is fair to say that recent biblical and historical scholarship has not brought about *more* agreement that only a supernatural intervention could explain the reports about Jesus that have come down to us through history. The kind of case that *can* be made regarding Jesus as uniquely revelatory of the divine reality depends, it seems to us, on far more subjective and uncertain considerations than the ones advanced by those who claim to possess objective evidence. These considerations provide the basis of what might be called a *subjective apologetic.*

Imagine the case of a person (say, Joan) who understands all the reasons for doubting her own belief in the uniqueness of Jesus' relationship with God but nevertheless finds herself inescapably drawn to that belief. What reasons might she give, even to herself, for this apparently stubborn disposition? Or rather, what reasons might she have for regarding her belief as rationally permissible, and not just as an irrational compulsion she might be better off suppressing? It seems to us that she might credibly settle on the following four:

First, Joan seems to encounter, in and through the New Testament documents, an individual she can't adequately capture under the headings of powerful prophet, good rabbi, or moral exemplar. She fully understands the ways in which, according to scholars, the Gospels have been composed from multiple, sometimes conflicting sources, and the narratives have been shaped by literary techniques. Yet she can't shake off the conviction that she here encounters something other than a brilliant literary fiction. She seems to catch glimpses in these documents of one who is powerfully permeated by the presence of God, one in whom "the fullness of God was pleased to dwell." It's as if, in her experience of reading about this individual, she is encountering a divine, or what Rudolf Otto would have called a "numinous," presence.[10] This experience gives her reason to think that the text somehow testifies to a unique revelation of God in history.

Joan's sense of these texts as authentic witnesses to the self-manifestation of God is enhanced, second, by what she herself experiences outside the context of reading and reflecting on the New Testament accounts. She knows that subjective religious experiences—whether they occur during prayer or on some life-changing occasion such as witnessing the death of a loved one—are fallible and that every person filters them through her own interpretive framework. Still, she cannot deny that *what* she experiences, in those moments that are to her most revelatory of the UR itself, seems to be the same God to whose presence and nature Jesus testified. Indeed, it is not just that the *content* of her religious experience matches the content of Jesus' teaching; it seems to her in such moments that she is directly experiencing the Spirit of Christ. Her subjective experience is not merely testifying to, or luring her toward, the kind of self-giving love that (she believes) Jesus manifested; that love actually seems present to her in her individual experience. Such experiences give her reason to believe that Jesus was not just one among many manifestations of God but was somehow God's unsurpassable revelation.

Third, Joan is well aware that Christians have not held identical beliefs through the entire history of Christianity. She knows that Christian faith is *semper reformata, semper reformans*, as the Reformation thinkers said: "always reformed, always reforming." Yet somehow, across all the centuries, she perceives a basic continuity of Christian belief and experience. However diverse their cultural and historical settings, participants in this tradition continually return to the biblical texts; they believe that in Jesus God was somehow powerfully manifest; they repeat a core message, a proclamation they have called the "kerygma" or gospel; and they share a hope for a future in which God plays a role. In one form or another, they affirm what we have called "the Christian proposition," that the infinite grace and compassion of the ultimate reality itself were present, and in some sense continue to be present, in this particular human being. They may speak of the one they experience in different ways—as the Holy Spirit, the Spirit of Christ, or the Resurrected One—but it is somehow "the same Lord" who is proclaimed. When, across this long tradition, Joan finds herself holding many of the same core beliefs and experiencing the divine reality in similar forms, she takes her faith to be further supported and strengthened.

A fourth argument is more philosophical in nature. It hearkens back to the intuitions about values and the UR that have repeatedly played a role in earlier chapters. When one conceives God as sharply distinct from the world, the task of conceiving God's possible involvement in the Jesus event—or any other revelatory event, for that matter— becomes proportionately more difficult. Yet throughout this book we have made the case for a participatory relationship of human and divine action, not just in moments of transformative divine action or human holiness, but as a defining feature of the created order.[11] On this participatory and panentheistic account, human values like justice and love both respond to and help shape the influence of divine values that are communicated to finite beings through what we have called the divine "lure."[12]

How does that account bear on the status of Jesus? According to the participatory theory of divine action we introduced in Chapter 3 and then developed further in Chapter 5, someone who is drawn to the Christian tradition and partakes of the religious experiences that tradition makes available to her has reason to think that Jesus of Nazareth responded to the divine lure in an unusually intense or complete fashion. Why should she suppose, however, that other religious leaders did not respond in equally valid ways? What reason, in other words, might Joan have to suppose that Jesus responded in a uniquely authoritative, indeed unsurpassable, way?

Suppose Joan holds the (for her) fundamental intuition that any adequate conception of the UR must include compassion as one of its central attributes. An ultimate reality that was not characterized by compassion in its highest form would not be one that she could worship, since for her it is axiomatic that whatever should turn out to be the religious ultimate will have a nature characterized by love. She then asks what this standard entails: what is required for us to speak of God as maximally compassionate? She concludes that divine love would count as involving compassion in this sense only if God was able somehow to share in the joys and the sufferings of God's creation. But, she reasons, for an infinite being to share in the joys and sufferings of finite beings, it would have to shed some of the qualities that we normally associate with infinity. Perhaps this means that it would have to limit itself voluntarily in some ways in order to experience compassion in the sense just described. Perhaps there would have to be a kind of divine self-emptying, without which God could not experience and manifest this ultimate good of compassion or love.

Joan knows that intuitions about the highest values vary. Although she can give reasons for this focus on self-emptying compassion, she recognizes that they will probably be persuasive only to those who share similar intuitions. This lowers the result of her reflection so far to level 3 in our schema above.

But there is one final step. Let's suppose that Joan cannot help but notice an extraordinary fit between (on one hand) her intuitions concerning the ultimate value of compassion and (on the other hand) the sayings and actions attributed to Jesus in the New Testament narratives. As we saw at the end of Chapter 6, a compelling account can be given of the relationship between divine compassion and Jesus' kenotic actions. There we described the self-giving love of Jesus as responding to and embodying the self-giving love of God. The link between the two, on this account, was more than circumstantial; Jesus' perfect obedience to God's will actually became identical with the divine compassion or love. After all, we noted, it is only if self-giving love for others accords with the will of God that such love on the part of a human being could constitute perfect obedience to God's will. And it is only if the two became identified in Jesus' actions that one can suppose that Jesus' obedience to God actually made *God's* infinite grace and compassion present to the world.

Joan is right to find some additional support for her belief in this convergence. And yet how can she know that no other human being ever manifested perfect self-giving love as fully as Jesus did? She *believes* that Jesus uniquely manifested divine grace and compassion; she has some reasons for her belief; and yet she cannot actually *demonstrate* this conclusion even to her own satisfaction. Her belief thus represents an instance of level-4 believing as we described it above.

But now suppose that, in addition to her belief in the uniqueness of Jesus' relation to the divine Spirit, Joan finds herself drawn to the traditional belief that, after his death on the cross, Jesus' body was miraculously restored to life in a newly powerful and immortal form, left his tomb, and appeared to his disciples. We have been assuming throughout this discussion that Joan accepts the account of divine action we presented in Chapter 3 and that served as a major premise of Chapters 5 and 6. On that assumption, Joan cannot claim to have reasons for the belief in a physical resurrection that we have just described—at least not reasons that render that belief rationally permissible, let alone rationally indicated, from the point of view of the relevant communities of inquiry. If she remains attached to it none-theless, she presumably regards it as something she *hopes* may yet turn out to be true, even though she lacks sufficient reason at present to believe it. Or perhaps she can no longer even *hope* that it may turn out to be true, in which case it becomes for her at best an inspiring fiction. In other words, it falls to level 5 or level 6 in our typology, the levels reserved for cases in which the agent either hopes the claim is true (but does not regard it as rationally permissible when judged against her other beliefs and the standards of any relevant communities of inquiry) or is content to use it as a metaphorical way of expressing what she does, in fact, believe about Jesus. In certain moments, for instance in the context of worship, she may allow herself to slip into something like a state of belief in the traditional claim, even while remaining tacitly aware of its (for her) nonliteral status.

Resurrection hope and the question of the Trinity

In the previous sections, we developed a scale of degrees or levels of rational justification. We then indicated where the various arguments and conclusions presented in earlier chapters seemed to fall along that scale.

In the process, we have in effect been sketching the boundaries of a Christian theological position that stands somewhere between the most liberal end of the spectrum, where one holds only those beliefs about Jesus that might be endorsed by any moderately theistic observer, and the most conservative or orthodox end, where one affirms without qualification the boldest Christian claims about the physical resurrection of Jesus and his unity ("hypostatic union") with God. On the position at which we have arrived, believers can give strong reasons for affirming that Jesus manifested the grace and compassion of the UR during his life and continued to do so after his death, as God acted in such a way as to make "the mind of Christ Jesus" present to the disciples and their followers. Indeed, those reasons are strong enough that, in our judgment, the communities with which Christians are in conversation should regard them as sufficient—not to "prove the resurrection," but at least to justify belief on the part of those who have certain kinds of intuitions and experiences.

For some, there are reasons to go a step further. Even after critical consideration of the arguments and objections on both sides, they still find themselves convinced that Jesus embodied the divine grace and compassion in a unique way and to an unsurpassable degree, and therefore that the authority of Jesus' mode of life has become the central focus of the divine "lure" in general, the core content of what the Spirit communicates to humanity as a whole. While their belief in the unique authority of Jesus is based on reasons that render it permissible in light of their other beliefs, they realize that those reasons are sufficiently controversial, ambiguous, and dependent on subjective experience that they can no longer expect an observer to endorse them, *even as reasons for them*. Hence the difference between these two kinds of Christian belief about Jesus corresponds to the difference between level 3 and level 4, respectively, on our epistemic scale.

At the end of the last section, we went on to consider the status of an additional claim, namely that Jesus rose bodily from his tomb and appeared to his disciples in bodily form. That claim turned out to be far more problematic than those considered earlier, at least for anyone who accepted the account of divine action we developed earlier in the book. Readers who accept our premises may still *hope* this additional belief is true. Insofar as it functions for them in the context of hope, or (alternatively) insofar as it serves as an important metaphor, perhaps guiding and orienting much of what they say and do, their attitude toward it resides at level 5 or level 6, respectively.

There are two traditional Christian beliefs, related to the ones we have just considered, to which we must return as we approach the end of our argument. Both have played a critical role in the history of Christian thought, and both have surfaced at various points in previous chapters. One is the claim that other human beings—on some accounts only believers, but on other accounts everyone—will in some sense participate, after their own earthly lives, in the post-mortem state of the "risen" Jesus. Another is that the uniqueness of Jesus' relationship with the ultimate reality extends to the point of metaphysical *identity* with that reality itself. The first of these is traditionally known as the hope of Resurrection; the second lies at the core of the traditional doctrine of the Trinity. How should these claims be understood in light of our larger argument, and where should they be placed along our epistemic scale?

In Chapter 3 and again in Chapter 6 we affirmed, as a corollary of belief in a benevolent God, the assumption that human beings— especially those who have been subjected to life-stunting poverty, disease, or injustice—must have an opportunity for continued existence beyond the grave. We noted how strange it would be to exclude Jesus from that "eschatological" hope; after all, he too was an innocent victim of human cruelty. From this point of view, the belief that the personhood of Jesus must in some sense have survived his execution would seem to be a well-justified belief. But is it as strongly justified as the position we have called minimally personalistic theism—justified, in other words, at level 2 in our typology? As we have shown, a somewhat lengthy chain of reasons connects the two. If all the links in the chain hold, the existence of a benevolent God and of unjustified suffering should entail some form of post-mortem recompense for the victims of injustice. But what if some of the links in this chain are weaker than others? What if there are objections to the various steps in the argument that scholars have not yet recognized? Since lengthy chains of inference increase the possibility of error, they should decrease one's claims to certainty. Hence belief in Jesus' post-mortem existence, though justified, remains an irreducibly controversial claim.

So much for degrees of certainty. One still wants to know exactly how one should understand Jesus' continuing existence as a particular person, one who enjoys an eschatological future that many hope to share. The answer, if there is one, must lie in the nature of a post-mortem existence in which personal identity is no longer defined and sustained by the conditions of physical embodiment. But if not in a body, more or less like the bodies we ourselves possess, where does the person, the subjectivity of Jesus continue to exist? If there is no longer a physical body to carry or sustain it, in what, or through what, is Jesus' personal existence, his subjective selfhood, maintained? Has he simply become a disembodied consciousness, subsisting by itself? That hypothesis would be as unsatisfying to the traditional believer in a bodily resurrection of Jesus as it would be to everyone who denies, with most contemporary scientists and philosophers, that it makes sense to imagine a finite consciousness existing on its own.

Here we arrive at a fundamental question: if Jesus continues to exist neither as a physically embodied individual nor as a disembodied consciousness, how should we suppose that his existence is actually sustained? In Chapter 5 we noted the near interchangeability, in Paul's Epistle to the Romans, of "Christ," the "Spirit of Christ," the "Spirit," and the "Spirit of God." Suppose we take a hint from this Pauline language and suggest that the continuing personal existence of Jesus was and is sustained directly by the agency of God—that is, directly by God's "Spirit." In other words, on this hypothesis, the Spirit of God itself takes on the role of sustaining the subjective existence of Jesus that Jesus' physical body played during his natural life. Jesus lives, but no longer as a separately embodied individual; instead, as Paul suggests in an especially evocative phrase, Jesus now "lives to God" (Romans 6:10).

But how could that be? How do we begin to make sense of the notion of one person, one mind, one subject, continuing to function within the embracing activity of another mind and another person? Persons as we know them are individuated and separated from each other precisely by the bodies they inhabit; the idea of one person transcending those boundaries and subsisting within another might seem to be the stuff of madness, or nightmare.

Theism in general only makes sense, however, if we can admit the possibility of a not-less-than-personal being whose self-sustaining infinitude by definition does not require the finite boundaries of embodied existence. It is not at all clear, for that reason, that the merging of a finite person with the unbounded agency of God creates the same kind of contradiction as the merging of two finite persons. Indeed, according to one important development in modern theology, albeit one with ancient roots, *every finite subject* exists within the infinite and encompassing subjectivity of the UR. This, again, is the theology of panentheism (from the Greek words *pan-en-theos*, meaning "all in God"), which has surfaced repeatedly in the preceding pages.[13] All persons, on this account, are sustained even in their physically embodied form by divine agency, and in fact it is the regular operation of divine agency that gives rise in the first place to what we call the laws of nature, and therefore to the existence of physical bodies themselves. From that point of view, the sustaining of Jesus' personhood directly by the divine Spirit can be seen as completing and perfecting what is already implicit in the relation of every finite person to his or her "ground" in the infinity of divine personhood.[14]

In the ordinary, pre-resurrected state, the bodies of finite persons are intermediaries, as it were, between the sustaining presence of God, without which the universe would not continue to exist from moment to moment, and their own subjective existence. In that sense, Jesus' resurrection may be seen to have involved the removal of this intermediate physical condition without which, according to the hypothesis defended in Chapter 3, human subjectivity could not have evolved in the first place. As we argued in that chapter, the regularities of physical existence, which we experience precisely because we exist in a physically embodied form, were necessary for the emergence of finite persons capable of knowing themselves as such. But once such persons existed, it could well be possible for them to continue existing in another state of existence—a future "cosmological epoch"—in which the conditions of physical existence as we know it in our universe might be transcended in ways we can only begin to imagine. If we already suppose that, even in her pre-resurrected state, a person's thoughts are ultimately grounded in divine agency, why should we refrain from hypothesizing that death might bring about new kinds of relations between human minds and their divine ground?

Consider, then, the possibility that the personhood of Jesus, after his death, was sustained directly by the Spirit of God. Does that hypothesis help explain how the kind of future the rest of us hope for is related to Jesus' eschatological existence? What makes this question hard to answer is that we have no experience of a state in which communication between persons is no longer mediated through the conditions of physical embodiment. One function of a physical body, after all, is to provide the discrete features that identify an individual agent and that both enable and limit the possibilities of her communication with others. But on the kind of participatory and panentheistic account we have been developing, the Spirit of God is what ultimately sustains all finite individuals in existence. Assuming that it is God "in whom we live and move and have our being" (Acts 17:29), and with the mediation of bodies replaced by the direct agency of the Spirit, there is no reason why God could not directly sustain the discrete features of particular persons after their deaths. The Pauline notion of a post-resurrection "spiritual body" (*sōma pneumatikon*, 1 Corinthians 15:44) would then mean a body directly sustained by the Spirit. Each finite person would have a distinct place within this universal Spirit as the distinctive being he or she is, but the medium of existence would now be not flesh and bone but the Spirit itself. Communion with God, and presumably also with others, would be much more direct than what we currently enjoy.

If one combines that speculation with the claims about Jesus we have explored both in the previous chapter and earlier in this one, it becomes easier to understand the traditional Christian picture of the risen Jesus as the center or "head" of an eschatological or "heavenly" community in which, thanks to the perfect conformity of his will to the will of God, his becomes the central, pervasively influential presence.

This conception of "resurrected" or eschatological existence not only suggests a way of explaining the relation between our future hope and the eschatological existence of Jesus; it also suggests an approach to the final major doctrine we have yet to address in this chapter, the Trinity. Consider for the moment just the first two "Persons" of the Trinity, traditionally termed the Father and the Son. With no finite body to separate the post-mortem Jesus from the one he called "the Father," and given their perfect conformity of wills, the two could indeed "be one" in this state (John 10:30), yet without eliminating the personal distinction between them. Moreover, it would be possible for other agents to be infused by and to seek to emulate their unity, "so that they may be one, as we are one" (John 17:11).

What about the "Third Person" of the Trinity as traditionally conceived, that is, the Holy Spirit? After Jesus' life and death, the New Testament describes a unique, limited period during which he was both "risen" and present on earth. After that time he would depart ("I am going to the Father," John 14:12). No longer personally present to his disciples, he would send "the Advocate, the Holy Spirit," who "will teach you everything, and remind you of all that I have said to you" (John 14:26).

The account we have been sketching is, we think, truer to this picture than are many of the accounts that have been part of popular Christian piety. The One who is immediately present to believers is the Holy Spirit. This Spirit "will not speak on his own" (John 16:13), but as "the Spirit of Christ" he reminds believers of who Jesus was and what he taught. In the beautiful words of the King James translation, he will "bring all things to your remembrance, whatsoever I have said unto you" (John 14:26). Put in more Trinitarian terms, one would say that the Spirit imparts to all future disciples a vision of the state of the unity of Father and Son, the sort of unity we described above. The earthly Jesus will not be personally present to believers but—to use the influential metaphor of the Apostle's Creed—will "sit at the right hand of the Father." But the Holy Spirit continuously shares in (and helps to constitute) the communion that Father and Son eternally enjoy and in which the other members of the heavenly community also participate. This communion is the final (eschatological) culmination of the life and mission of the one who said "not my will, but thine be done." Thus, insofar as the Spirit conveys the communion of Father and Son, it also conveys the mind of Christ to human beings who have not yet entered the eschatological state.

What status should we assign to such theories about the post-mortem state and authority of Jesus, and about where he finally stands in relation to God? Certainly there are traditional extensions of such possibilities—for instance, the claim that Jesus even during his earthly life was the incarnation of a preexistent divine being, the Son of God, who was united from all eternity with the other two Persons of the Trinity—which are more difficult to describe and justify to the relevant communities of experts (and perhaps even to oneself). By contrast, the eschatological and theological picture that we have just outlined *does* seem to follow, without too many intervening steps, from conclusions that seem to us to be justified or at least permissible.

Once again, however, the inherent fallibility of extended chains of inference must be considered as well. This version of a Trinitarian theology has a certain explanatory strength and avoids difficulties with which other accounts have struggled. These are good reasons to endorse it. But given the inherently complex and controversial nature of *any* speculation on the nature of the UR, and especially speculation that must link history, textual study, and metaphysical reflection, it makes more sense to speak of reasons that make belief permissible than of proofs that compel assent.

Before we close, we should mention one final belief that has played and continues to play an important role in the religious lives of many Christians: a belief we discussed in Chapter 6, where we introduced it as the personal but nonphysical theory of Jesus' post-mortem presence. This is the theory that, after Jesus' death, the Spirit of God made the person or subject Jesus—and not just the "mind" or attitude, or even (as above) the ongoing eschatological reality of Jesus—present to the disciples and has continued to make him present to believers ever since. Hence Jesus himself is personally and subjectively present, albeit in a nonphysical form, whenever and wherever the Spirit of God communicates with human minds.

Our consideration of this theory in Chapter 6 revealed some challenging problems. It was hard to see how a Jesus who was personally present to (and actively communicating with) millions of people simultaneously, and who had continued to be present in this sense without a break over thousands of years, could be the same kind of entity as a finite person—the same person, say, who dined with his disciples or remembered living in his family home in Nazareth. Somehow, if this theory is true, Jesus' resurrection must have involved a transition from finite to infinite personhood. But such a transition brings with it weighty philosophical problems: is the post-mortem

Jesus really identical with (that is, the same person as) the pre-mortem Jesus? What theory of personhood could explain an identity that straddles both finite and infinite personhood? How can one be transformed from a finite to an infinite person and yet continue to count as the *same* person? Indeed, does the notion of a finite person who is at the same time infinite even make sense?

Faced with these questions, one may well ask whether belief in Jesus' ongoing personal but nonphysical presence is even rationally *permissible*, let alone fully justified. In terms of the levels of justification we sketched in the previous section, this amounts to the question of whether such a belief should be placed on level 4 or perhaps relegated to level 5 or 6. Is it something a rational agent can permissibly believe, or only something she can hope is true, or perhaps treat as a suggestive metaphor?

That question, however, can be very misleading, for a reason that applies to our entire account of the multiple ways in which a rational agent can be committed to any particular religious claim. In the case of Christian claims per se, as one moves beyond the claim of Jesus' uniqueness into the more speculative theological and eschatological territory we have been exploring in this section, it becomes increasingly difficult to say where a given claim stands or *ought* to stand, even from one's own subjective point of view.

A strong theory of the Trinity, asserting a metaphysical identity of Father and Son as two "hypostases" of one substance, and a strongly personalistic version of the claim that Jesus is present to believers would both appear to be instances of claims whose status is ambiguous in this way. Neither, after all, is positively ruled out by the account of the UR or the theory of divine action we developed earlier in this book. Nor can we exclude the possibility that someone else may find a way to solve the conceptual problems they seem to us to raise. Are these claims, then, that one may find oneself actually believing, perhaps with the kind of rational permissibility that would place them at level 4 in our schema? Or are they possibilities that one only *hopes* may be true and that, on the basis of that hope, one uses to guide one's thoughts and actions? Or, again, are they best conceived as powerful metaphors for the importance of the role that Jesus plays in the believer's engagement with ultimacy?

These questions are a reminder that our epistemic "levels" are really just convenient points along a continuum and that, for any individual believer, the location of any particular claim along that continuum is subject to revision in light of new arguments, new experiences, and new discoveries. One can say with some confidence, at any particular moment, which claims appear to be better justified than others, but one must also acknowledge the ongoing religious and theoretical attraction of claims that one cannot, at the moment, find fully convincing. The upshot is a necessary humility and an openness to the claims of the tradition—and the criticisms of those outside it—that, in our view, belong to the essence of what is traditionally known as a life of faith.

8

The spectrum of belief and the question of the church

In the foregoing pages, we have worked our way through some of the most serious reasons for doubt faced by those attracted to religious belief, and to Christian versions of religious belief in particular. The result has been (what we think is) a compelling view of the ultimate reality (UR), the relation of human beings to that reality, and the role of one particular human being in the development of that relationship.

Our constructive proposals reflect a struggle with these objections that preceded our work on this book and in some cases stretched over quite a number of years. Answers that seemed to satisfy the objections were subjected to the most rigorous scrutiny possible, exposed to further criticism and revised accordingly. In that sense, the many answers tried out and rejected in the previous pages are fossils of once living hypotheses that failed to stand up to criticism.

The book that has resulted from that process actually contains two narratives, intricately connected, that run from beginning to end. One tells the emerging story of a form of Christian belief that (we believe) overcomes the most serious objections in the literature. The other traces a gradual progression from more "objective" conclusions—those on which experts in a given field will or should generally agree—to conclusions that are deeply dependent on an individual's particular experiences and assumptions (see the series of "levels" described in the previous chapter). Both critics and defenders of religious faith often fail to acknowledge the way the very nature of the arguments changes as one moves from general philosophical to highly specific confessional claims. This change has everything to do with how one understands the nature and role of religious communities today.

The necessity—and costs—of revision

Some readers will be surprised that we have retained so much of traditional Christian belief; others disappointed (or worse) by our abandonment of claims they regard as essential to the tradition's intellectual integrity, religious power, or both. We affirm the not-less-than-personal nature of the infinite reality who is the ground of all existence; in fact, we regard that affirmation as rationally indicated for all inquirers—or, more exactly, as rationally preferable to the alternatives. We also affirm the uniquely authoritative role of Jesus of Nazareth in determining the relation of that divine reality to human beings, although we do not assert that this affirmation has the same rational claim on other rational agents.

At the same time, we stop short of affirming a number of the most dramatic traditional claims—for instance, that God miraculously intervenes with some frequency to alter the natural course of events within the created universe; that Jesus rose bodily from the grave; or that the finite human being Jesus was and is identical to one of the infinite and eternal "Persons" constituting the divine reality itself. We do not *deny* those claims exactly, but our reflections on the reasons for doubt outlined in the first chapter continue to prevent us from affirming them. In the end, we affirm a set of conclusions that most observers would regard as remaining within the realm not only of theistic but also of specifically Christian propositions. But even the traditional claims we retain emerge in a somewhat altered form.

In that sense, Christian minimalism as we understand it involves the *revision* of certain beliefs that have played a major role in the history of Christianity (although it is easy to overlook the passionate disagreements that have marked the development of Christian teachings since their inception). Revision entails a certain cost. In the first place, some will say that granting the need for any revision calls into question the validity of the tradition as a whole: if this tradition really is the right place to look for the truth about the UR, why should its teachings change over time? And why should people continue to stake their lives on a tradition whose claims are subject to revision in the light of new information? There is also a specifically *religious* cost: how can one continue to be moved, inspired, and spiritually uplifted by an ancient miracle story that has now been revised in a way that downplays or even removes the dimension of miracle, at least as miracles are conventionally understood?

The answers that individuals give to these questions vary greatly. But the dilemma they imply is not merely faced by a small number of hypercritical inquirers; it confronts all who regard themselves as part of the Christian tradition today.

Take just one of the challenges believers wrestle with: the problem of evil. One can affirm that God sets aside natural laws and directly causes events in the world. But a God who does such things could, by similar means, also intervene to save an innocent child from a monstrous predator. Yet in countless cases God does *not* act to save innocent lives or prevent innocent suffering; and one who can prevent innocent suffering but fails to do so would appear to be responsible for that suffering.

This apparently unavoidable conclusion confronts believers with a difficult dilemma. They can affirm in faith that "God has his reasons" and let the questioning stop there. Indeed, this Job-like response is often presented as the only acceptable Christian answer: God sometimes intervenes and sometimes doesn't, and faith requires that one not ask any further questions. Or a believer can try to conceive God's relationship with the world in ways that remove the apparent inconsistency. Struggling with the question of innocent suffering and trying to find reasonable answers does not eliminate the need for faith and trust; far from it. But it does presuppose that it is acceptable—and for some of us, indispensable—to face these grounds for doubt head-on and, if possible, find adequate ways of answering them. This is a difficult and, at times, a costly endeavor. Still, we suggest, to bypass the difficulties completely, or to exempt oneself from any obligation to give a reasonable account of one's faith, is even more costly, because it leaves one with no reason to suppose that it really makes sense to hold the beliefs one actually holds.

Many regard challenges like the problem of evil as purely theoretical, but in fact they have significant implications for how one lives out one's faith. In this chapter we hope to show that a viable life of Christian faith is still possible for those who are concerned about the most serious objections of our day—those stemming from science, the problem of evil, religious plurality, contemporary biblical scholarship, and certain traditional claims, like the reports of Jesus' resurrection, that are inherently as well as irreducibly controversial. Indeed, for a growing number of believers in our day there is no alternative but to grapple with these intellectual challenges and to make what seem to be the necessary revisions. What does faith look like for such persons? What kinds of Christian community can survive the predicament of belief, and how should members of such communities interact with those whose beliefs differ from their own?

The life of faith

It is time to specify what kind of religious life—what kind of "life of faith"—might be implied by the interpretation of Christian claims we developed in Chapters 5 and 6 and then reprised in the latter part of Chapter 7. In fact, we have presented three different ways of interpreting what may actually have occurred in the events that Christians regard, rather astonishingly, as the climactic self-revelation, within human history, of the UR itself.

In one sense, these three interpretations are closely linked. They all see the resurrection of Jesus as a profoundly and literally *spiritual* event: an event, that is, in which God really does act but in which the divine action takes place through God's influence on human minds and not through a miraculous suspension of natural laws. According to the first of these theories, the "participatory," the divine Spirit presents to human minds the self-surrendering mode of being that Jesus exemplified, along with the opportunity to share that mode of being and the divine–human relationship that it expresses and on which it depends. According to the second theory, the one we called "Spirit-centered" (or "pneumatological"), the Spirit itself takes on a Jesuanic character and thereafter makes present the authority of Jesus as the one whose perfect obedience to God became the unsurpassable revelation of God's own infinite grace and compassion. On the third or "personal presence" theory, Jesus himself continues to be personally although nonphysically present through the Spirit to believers, and perhaps to human beings in general.

The third of these interpretations accords the most fully with traditional Christian claims and forms of worship. Indeed, many see it as an entailment (or ground) of the claim that the UR is "triune" in nature. It also promises an unparalleled intimacy of relationship between divine and human realities, and that promise no doubt accounts for its spiritual and emotional power. For that reason, it remains a focus of belief for many Christians, and it can be an object of fascination and hope even for those who cannot manage actually to believe it, or who can only do so in relatively rare moments of religious experience and conviction.

The first interpretation—the participatory theory—is the easiest to explain and defend. It provides a reasonable resting place for those who cannot believe, or at least cannot continuously believe, the more robust traditional alternatives. And yet it too reflects core Christian convictions, and it too can be sufficient to motivate a life of faith (though perhaps in ways that are difficult for more traditional believers to see). In affirming the possibility of participating in God through Jesus' self-surrendering love, it offers a mode of existence in which human self-transcendence meets, and even shares in, the compassion and freedom of the divine reality itself. For some, at least, belief in the reality of that offer will be enough.

It makes complete sense, then—religiously as well as rationally—to believe the participatory theory. It makes sense, that is, for someone who accepts the arguments we have presented in the foregoing pages and who has experienced the presence of divine grace and compassion in the Christian tradition and its testimony to the significance of Jesus.

But what if such a person feels drawn to *something more*, something closer to the proposition that Jesus uniquely and unsurpassably embodied divine grace, or even that Jesus, after his death, continued to be personally present to his followers in some form? What if she finds herself, at least on occasion, believing that one of these stronger claims is actually true? How should she interpret her own belief, whether enduring or occasional, when it seems to her to lack the kinds of reasons she would dearly like it to have?

Persons in this situation may experience an ongoing tension between the more readily defensible claims of the participatory theory and their attraction to the possibility that claims of Jesus' unique authority or ongoing personal presence may be true after all. They may even find themselves oscillating, perhaps on a daily basis, between stronger and weaker forms of Christian belief. At times, perhaps, the participatory theory will seem to have stopped just sort of a vital truth;

at other times, the presence of Jesus will slip into the status of something hoped for but not actually believed in. At still other times, the
Spirit-centered theory of the resurrection will seem to occupy a
reasonable middle ground, since from this vantage point the strongest
traditional claims make at least metaphorical sense and the picture of
divine action that is least vulnerable to the problem of evil remains
intact.

It is important to notice, however, that despite the tensions and
oscillations believers may experience, all three of these theories are
interpretations of a single larger claim, the one we have called "the
Christian proposition": that the infinite grace and compassion of the
UR itself were present, and *in some sense* continue to be present, in this
particular human being. Furthermore, all three theories share a commitment to the notion that Jesus' ongoing significance is not just a
matter of religious symbolism, not just a projection of human imagination, but a manifestation of the active role and engagement of the
divine Spirit itself. That shared commitment sets all three apart from
the more reductive or (as they are more often labeled) "liberal"
interpretations that, early in Chapter 5, we called the symbolic and
exemplary theories. Even if one continues to oscillate among these
three alternatives, the range of one's oscillation is at least confined to a
family of views that clearly fall within the spectrum of Christian belief.
For that reason, the fact that one may believe one theory while hoping
one of the others may turn out to be true after all should not be an
obstacle to what is traditionally called a life of faith.

For many, religious experience will play an irreducible role in
inclining them toward (or away from) one or more of these responses.
Early in Chapter 5, we mentioned that those who had experienced the
presence of God through their encounter with the New Testament
testimony about Jesus would have a particular interest in the possible
truth of those claims. But they may also have something else: an
abiding sense of divine presence and love that remains intact even
when they find themselves compelled to revise their original understanding of that testimony.

Of course it is always possible that someone's understanding of the
experiences that initially moved and enveloped her will gradually
change to the point where they lose their spiritual power and even
their grip on her interest and attention. It is possible, in other words,
for people to lose their faith. Indeed, they may sometimes lose it as a

result of rational inquiry into the same claims that elicited that faith in the first place. We do not deny, then, that revision can be costly indeed! For others, however, the power of their original experience, and their ability to recover that power or to continue drawing on it, will enable them to tolerate a good deal of oscillation in their particular beliefs without the constant worry that the next argument they encounter will deprive them altogether of a life of faith.

Theory to practice

Having reached certain conclusions about what to believe (in spite of all the reasons for doubt), we can now apply them to the practical questions of how an individual believer should live her life, and—since it is part of the same question—how communities of such believers might incorporate this book's conclusions into their understanding of themselves and their relationships to other religious and nonreligious traditions.

Of course our practical recommendations will have to reflect the minimalism of our theoretical conclusions. We began this inquiry with an interest in questions of ultimacy, an attraction to the claims of Christianity, and perhaps above all an attraction to Christianity's central figure as portrayed in its founding texts. But we also began with a set of powerful doubts (shared, we believe, by many) about the truth of those claims. The path this book's argument has taken, including all the smaller and larger conclusions we have reached along the way, is just one among multiple paths of reflection that might plausibly be followed by someone beginning from the same starting point. Not surprisingly, we think the best reasons are on the side of taking the particular turns we did, and continuing as we have where others might have paused. But, with a few exceptions, we have not claimed that ours were the only reasonable choices, or that someone who failed to proceed in the same direction or travel the same distance was thereby making a rational or moral mistake. We recognize that even those who accept our premises might reach other conclusions.

We also recognize that those who do *not* share our starting point will diverge even more strongly from what we recommend. As we saw in Chapter 4, those whose engagement with the UR has been shaped by non-Christian traditions may have equally good reasons to reach conclusions that reflect their own, very different, experiences and points of departure. In Chapter 7, we showed why even those who hold Christian assumptions may do so with very different kinds or degrees of commitment. For all those reasons, it would be an act of hubris, to say the least, to prescribe the exact forms of individual or collective life that an engagement with the UR must take.

And there is still another reason why our practical recommendations will have to be advanced in a tentative as well as a minimalistic spirit. Perhaps the single most important hypothesis in this entire book is that divine action within the created universe is and must be *participatory*— that is, that God and God's creatures together shape both the form and the content of divine communication with finite beings, including those salient moments of communication that constitute what is traditionally known as divine "revelation." If revelation itself is a combined product of divine and human agency, so too will be the human practices that respond to it.

These considerations all count against the notion that one could derive a single blueprint for all individual or collective practice from the kind of reflection exemplified by the preceding seven chapters. And the task of deciding what *does* follow from such reflection becomes further complicated when one considers the actual social and institutional context of contemporary Christian practice.

Christianity today

A major national survey recently published in *USA Today* shows that 72 percent of "Millennials"—Americans between the ages of 18 and 29—now consider themselves "spiritual but not religious."[1] Even among those who identify themselves as practicing Christians, the study shows that all the traditional forms of Christian practice have sharply declined from previous years, including church attendance, Bible study, and prayer. Doubts are sharper, and affiliation with institutional churches has dramatically decreased.

The decline of traditional churches may well continue, so that within a decade or so the effects may be almost as widespread in the United States as they currently are in northern Europe. (On a typical Sunday, for example, only 0.5 percent of Germans attend church.)

Over the next ten to fifteen years, it has been predicted, more than half of all American mainline churches may close their doors; many others will struggle on without a full-time pastor. Denominations will continue to merge just so they can maintain even reduced national staffs and programs.

We have elsewhere published an account of these trends, analyzing the causes of the decline in participation in traditional churches;[2] those causes include the following:

(1) Church attendance is no longer socially necessary, that is, necessary for the social health and perhaps even the economic survival of individuals and their families, in contrast to earlier eras in which, especially in smaller communities, churches provided the main context for social interaction and were necessary to the relationships on which careers and businesses depended.

(2) By and large, people no longer believe that church attendance provides the only or the most important means of establishing and maintaining a sufficiently strong connection with God, however such a connection is specifically understood (for example, in terms of salvation, spiritual health, a life of meaning, etc.). An increasing number of Americans believe they can pursue their spiritual interests without the need of teaching by, or guidance from, a religious community.

(3) The dramatically increased mobility of individuals and families, as well as the decreased stability of family units, makes it harder to develop extended or cross-generational ties to any particular church.

(4) Communities are not only in continual flux; they are far more diverse in beliefs, values, and social identities than they were in earlier eras. This makes it harder to assemble or maintain congregations with sufficient critical mass, at least without embracing a greater degree of social and ideological diversity than some members can tolerate.

In short, the social conditions and beliefs that once motivated and sustained church attendance have been severely eroded in recent decades, and many religious institutions are crumbling as a result. In light of these developments, which embrace most of Europe and North America, the kind of reflection this book has exemplified may look like a case of fiddling while Rome burns (along with Wittenberg, Geneva, and Canterbury). We suggest, however, that the main conclusions reached above actually offer a useful—even hopeful—response to the crisis we have just described. That response takes the form of a minimalist, but still clearly Christian, understanding of church (the traditional term is "ecclesiology") that reflects the minimalism of our other conclusions.

Churches

One important feature of the minimalism we have developed in this book has been the recognition that different persons can quite properly and rationally stand in varying and changing relations to the claims of the religious traditions in which they find themselves or to which they are attracted. That recognition has major implications for the communities that preserve and embody those traditions. Those implications are often not openly acknowledged. Perhaps those responsible for leading and guiding the communities in question fear the consequences for themselves and their charges of too frankly acknowledging their own uncertainties. But, at least for some believers, not engaging reasons for doubt and the necessity of revision has costs of its own.

How, then, should one rethink the nature of religious community in this context? What does a "church" look like when reconceived in ways that respond to the conclusions of our earlier chapters and also, potentially, to the widespread decline of traditional congregations? What kind or kinds of religious community are likely to serve the needs of those who arrive at (roughly) the same theological conclusions we do?

To begin with, such a community will invite the participation of all who find themselves attracted to the teachings, actions, or personality of Jesus, as portrayed in the biblical accounts, re-imagined by later interpreters, and/or reconstructed by historical scholarship. It will not matter where the participants locate themselves along the spectrum of beliefs and other attitudes we surveyed in Chapter 7, or even whether they regard themselves as "Christians." Membership will not require or be defined by a literal adherence to any particular interpretation of the ultimate reality, or of Jesus' relation to that reality.

There are multiple reasons why so radical an openness seems warranted if not indeed unavoidable. First, the sources of doubt we sketched in our opening chapter are too powerful to be overcome or laid to rest with the kind of confidence that characterized, say, American Protestant churches in their most triumphant phase. Second, metaphysical and theological questions are inherently controversial, and metaphysical and theological answers, even when one has reason to consider them preferable to their alternatives, are too tentative and unstable to serve as communal boundaries in the way creeds and confessions formerly did. A third point is that an individual who fully appreciates the first two points is likely to find herself shifting, over time, along the spectrum of belief, sometimes believing a confessional claim without reservation, at other times regarding it as, at best, a powerful metaphor for something else.

Individuals of the sort we have in mind may be able on occasion, perhaps even for extended periods, to make themselves at home in congregations defined by adherence to creeds or confessions, but they may not be able to do so permanently or, in the long run, comfortably. When their doubt and uncertainty distance them from religious communities that are defined by tight doctrinal boundaries, statistics show that they are likely to join the growing ranks of the unchurched and semichurched who increasingly define the religious landscape not only of Europe but of the ostensibly more religious United States—or else seek new kinds of Christian communities that are no longer defined or structured in traditional ways.

What might hold a Christian community together when fixed creedal boundaries no longer define it? Clearly, if what its members believe plays *no* role at all, nothing will distinguish this community from others that engage in charitable actions and encourage the spiritual or moral growth of their participants.

We earlier recalled the "Christian proposition": again, that the infinite grace and compassion of the UR itself were present, and in some sense continue to be present, in a particular human being, namely, Jesus of Nazareth. We now wish to argue that a shared focus on this core proposition is sufficient to define a community of Christian life and worship. For reasons that have now become clear, the community can and should be open to all who are attracted to Jesus, so understood, even when they do not stand in a position of continuous and undoubting belief in the Christian proposition. Although for many it will be an object of belief, others will be continually attracted to it but will still stop short of explicitly affirming it. As in the early Christian communities that Paul worked with, this new community may include robust believers, those hanging onto their belief by the skin of their teeth, genuine seekers, permanent questioners, and those attracted to the central proposition but (apparently) incapable of fully affirming it.

In short, the kind of community we have in mind will be more complex than many Christian leaders would be prepared to countenance. But one should not be surprised by that outcome when one considers that, in a pluralistic, multicultural, and multireligious society, the question of personal identity in general has become significantly more complex than it was, say, 100 years ago. If this is true of the persons who join them, why would we expect that religious communities would have the sort of monolithic identities they may have had a century ago?

In traditional ecclesiologies, acceptance of the core doctrines of the church was expected to motivate an adherence to an accepted list of values. Those who first engaged in right belief and then right action could be admitted to membership. For many today, however, this order is reversed. Participating in a church community and beginning to share its values becomes a path toward belief rather than a consequence of what one already believes. (In one author's pithy expression, "believe, behave, belong" is replaced by "belong, behave, believe.")[3] A range of people—those attracted to the Christian proposition, those who clearly affirm it, and those with even more robust affirmations of the unique revelation of God through Jesus Christ—join together in a community associated with Jesus' name. They seek to live in ways consistent with his life and teachings, even while doubts may remain unresolved and the exact implications of his teachings only gradually become clear. Out of the evolving practices of worship, study, and discipleship, some degree of shared belief may well emerge, even if complete convergence of belief is unlikely.

Not surprisingly, in many cases the resulting *modes* of belief will be different from traditional believing. A distinguishing feature of our age is a need on the part of many people to reflect not just on what they affirm but also on *how* and in what sense they affirm it. The six levels of belief discussed in the previous chapter provide some sense of how wide the range of options is. "Hope-plus-faith" or "metaphorical belief" or "behaving as if," although not without their traditional analogs, define the spaces of belief and near-belief for many of those most strongly attracted to Christianity today.

In Chapter 1 we stressed two aspects of Christian minimalism that differentiated it from traditional belief: differences in the *content* of what one believes, and differences in the *manner* in which one believes. The last three chapters have spelled out the range of possible beliefs in some detail. Even in cases that clearly count as actual believing (those cases located at levels 2, 3, and 4 in the previous chapter), there are still differences from the nature of Christian believing as it tended to occur in the premodern world. Today's believer may be more open to alternatives; may hold her belief in a hypothetical mode; may vacillate between clear belief and hope-plus-faith; or may combine belief and doubt in many complex ways.

These subtle changes in how people believe are likely to affect, and indeed probably *should* affect, the nature of Christian community. Imagine an individual (say, Thomas) who recognizes that the only form of religious belief that is a live option for him is Christianity. Christian discipleship, striving to live in what he takes to be a Christ-like way, is central to his identity, but it is accompanied by great uncertainty about which traditional Christian doctrines, if any, are actually true. Thomas is not always sure what parts of the Christian tradition are divinely revealed and what parts are cultural accretions. Because of the complexity of his own religious attitudes, he approaches the beliefs of other traditions with great openness and tolerance. Hence, even though he knows he is unlikely ever to convert to another religion, he cannot assume that all other beliefs are false. Those who, like Thomas, have nontraditional attitudes toward other religions and toward those still seeking a religion—perhaps because they recognize something of themselves in these "seekers"—will form (and in fact are already forming) Christian communities with distinctly different forms of worship, different attitudes toward belief, and sometimes different beliefs as well.[4]

Finally, emerging forms of Christian community, whether they occur within traditional churches or in house churches or other alternative settings, develop not only new attitudes but also distinctively new forms of Christian practice. Leaders are no longer, or not only, teachers and proclaimers but conveners and hosts. Meetings may be held in nontraditional places, and address nontraditional topics in nontraditional formats.[5] Discussions are often complex and deeply theological; they encourage participants to respond to the classic Christian questions, but they are less likely to settle on a single response or make it a requirement for continuing participation in the community.

Using Christian language in a multireligious context

The kind of Christian community we have just been describing departs in significant ways from the traditional models. Yet it shares with them an abiding attachment to the core Christian proposition, an attachment that continues to distinguish it from communities belonging to other religions. In Chapter 4 we explored the implications of a world in which believers in any particular vision of the UR cannot ignore the existence of those with sharply differing visions. The question that now arises is what a Christian community organized along the lines we have suggested should say about, and to, communities with fundamentally different orientations.

The answer cannot be a simple denial that the differences matter. Even those who are most keenly aware of religious plurality can still affirm that there are more and less adequate ways of conceiving the UR to which all religions strive to respond. One cannot try, coherently, to engage any reality—ultimate or not—while asserting that every way of doing so is just as good as every other way! For that reason, we cannot follow the radically pluralistic prescriptions of John Hick and his followers.[6]

At the same time, a community of the kind we have in mind will practice the greatest possible humility in asserting and defending its reasons for pursuing the path it has chosen. The range of believing and nonbelieving responses we have identified may not have been fully available to Christian communities in earlier generations—in no small measure because they believed, or at least many did, that the eternal fate of each human being depended on the correctness of her beliefs, and indeed that the cost of error could be eternal damnation.

Now that such beliefs have declined among younger believers, even within conservative churches, radical humility and tolerance of religious difference are no longer signs of indifference to the fate of others (as they once seemed) but the inescapable moral and, arguably, *religious* obligations of those communities that fully appreciate both the reasons for doubt and the positive implications of the Christian proposition itself. According to that proposition, the best clue we have to the nature of the UR is the self-giving love of the one whose remembered words and actions draw and hold the Christian community's attention. Hence a Christian community of the sort we have in mind will necessarily enter into dialogue with its non-Christian counterparts in a spirit of deep humility, self-criticism, and respect.

But the problem of religious plurality has a further dimension we have not yet addressed. The question is not only how Christian communities should interact with those who do not share their commitment to the Christian proposition. More deeply, it is the question of how Christian communities should handle their own internal plurality, that is, the wide range of beliefs and belief-like commitments held by their own members. After considering the use of Christian language in dialogue with non-Christian communities, we must ask: what about the use of Christian language *within* Christian communities themselves? The kind of church we have described, after all, is a highly pluralistic one, distinguished from its more traditional predecessors by the widely varying levels of belief that openly and explicitly coexist within it. How will its members talk to each other, and how will they engage in the kinds of shared discourse that are so important (or at least traditionally have been) to practices like collective prayer and worship?

One guiding principle is to follow one of the simplest and most striking injunctions attributed to Jesus: "be not anxious."[7] Once we know that members of the community will be uttering any given proposition with widely varying attitudes—some literally believing, some merely hoping, some suspending disbelief, some using the language only as metaphor—there is no longer any point in trying to pin down the precise sense in which a confessional statement, as voiced collectively, is being or should be used by the community as a whole. The recital of a collective prayer (if that is still a part of the community's practice) should no longer provoke worries about potential mystification, bad faith, or peer pressure.

At the same time, those in a teaching role will have an obligation, it seems to us, to make sure they are not glossing over doubts and disagreements when they employ traditional formulas or quote from scripture. It would be absurd, of course, to suggest that every phrase in a sermon should be restated to indicate the exact sense in which the preacher understands it; sermons are not seminars, after all, but acts of inspiration and engagement. But the process of collective discussion and discovery—the movement we described earlier toward a *possible* agreement on what to believe and how to respond accordingly—can proceed only if the participants are honest about the differences they hope to transcend. Here again, the enemy to be overcome is anxiety: the fear that acknowledging differences will weaken the community and ultimately divide it. But that should not be a worry in a community that begins by honestly embracing its members' reasons for doubt.

Does it matter?

A few years ago the well-known theologian John B. Cobb, Jr., spoke to an annual conference of the United Church of Christ, a mainline Protestant denomination. He offered a perceptive analysis of the situation in American churches today:

> The more progressive denominations on the whole have been losing members and resources. There are many reasons. But I think the deepest one may be that what we do and say does not seem to be terribly important. This is true with regard to our children whom we bring up in the church. They may have a positive attitude toward it, but they may not see any reason to give much, if any, of their time and energy to its support.[8]

Religions function, among other things, to provide their adherents with a sense of meaningfulness, of being "at home in the universe." In Peter Berger's striking phrase, theological beliefs provide a "sacred canopy" that shields believers from anomie.[9] When a religious tradition no longer serves this purpose, people may still participate in its communities for cultural, aesthetic, or social reasons, but it loses its urgency and importance as an organizing principle in their lives.

In premodern Europe, the existence of a divine reality underlying and enveloping the natural world was so obvious to most people—it accorded so much with common sense—that it was experienced more as an ordinary fact than as a specifically religious assumption. (The very idea of "religions" as bodies of belief distinct from more ordinary and uncontroversial ways of responding to the world was not developed until the seventeenth century.) Until quite recently, Christian theologies provided believers with powerful justifications for personal, communal, and even national action. Practicing various forms of abstinence, worshiping and tithing, evangelizing or engaging in social activism, even waging war against one or another "evil empire"—all these were justified on theological grounds that many found deeply persuasive.

Churches have persisted, but in recent years the reasons for concrete action that churches once offered have ceased to be persuasive even for many of those who continue to attend them. It seemed at first that this was a problem only for so-called liberal churches, but the recent data show similar patterns among those who identify themselves as evangelical. The problem is especially evident when it comes to theological justifications for collective action. By contrast, the theologies that move people today tend to be more private and personal. They focus on personal salvation or individual experience, and by and large they tend to separate the church from the wider world.

The fault—if fault it is—does not lie solely with church leaders. Individuals in a complex, pluralistic society have multiple interests and commitments that variously shape and define their identity as religious and nonreligious agents. Indeed, they increasingly have multiple *religious* identities as well. Traditionally, churches were havens where those with a clear religious identity and a specified set of beliefs met to worship, to teach and be taught, and to carry out the activities consistent with those beliefs.

When church leaders can no longer presuppose a securely shared fabric of beliefs, they rely increasingly on extrinsic motivations: professional musicians, high-tech services, attractive social programs, and the like. The trouble is that reflective persons recognize that such initiatives are no longer tied to compelling and persuasive beliefs about what is ultimately the case. When those beliefs becomes *merely* metaphorical or poetic—or worse, when one finds oneself using language one no longer believes but vaguely feels that one *ought* to believe—one begins to wonder about the *raison d'être* of the entire institution and its practices. Is it surprising that many have the sense that (in John Cobb's words) "what we do and say does not seem to be terribly important"?

The proposals offered in this book are not intended—and are certainly not sufficient—to restore the kind of theological consensus, even at the level of a single congregation, that would give belonging to a church the practical urgency it once enjoyed. On the contrary, we have sought to describe what church communities will be like when they honestly acknowledge the absence of consensus and consciously invite and embrace those whose responses to the Christian proposition fall along the entire typology of levels described in Chapter 7. As we've suggested, these will be religious communities where "seekers"— persons lacking actual or at least consistent belief in core Christian claims—may study, pray, and worship alongside others whose beliefs are much more settled. Those whose religious practice is motivated by no more than "hope-plus-faith" (level 5) will be welcomed, as will those who oscillate between more and less robust forms of Christian belief.

Such communities may lack, at least initially, the unity of belief and purpose of more traditional churches. But at least they will be grounded in an honest acknowledgment of the reasons for doubting traditional claims and the multiplicity of ways in which believers take such reasons into account. Nor will they seek the kind of easy but shallow consensus that results from simply ignoring the tradition's more controversial claims. In that sense, they may help prepare the way for the possible emergence of a deeper consensus that will once again provide a basis of concerted thought and action.

The institutional possibilities we have sketched in this chapter indicate some of the settings in which Christian minimalists may in the meantime continue to participate in communities of prayer, reflection, and worship—even those minimalists who find themselves "no longer at ease" in congregations defined by traditional creeds or confessions.[10] We have argued that a community that recognizes the multiple and shifting states of belief and doubt in its members should take that reality into account when designing its educational programs and even, to some degree, when reflecting on the appropriate shape of its worship and other ceremonies.

One thing is clear, though. If the conclusions reached in earlier chapters are valid, one would expect that Christian worship will continue to focus, and perhaps even intensify its focus, on the self-surrendering obedience of Jesus as a reflection, even an embodiment of the self-giving love that characterizes the not-less-than-personal ground and source of existence that Jesus regarded as his "father." Christian praxis—that is, the work of the churches and of individual believers in responding to the needs of those around them—will be grounded not only in the mutual love of the "Father" and the "Son" but in the recognition that divine love and justice can only operate through the medium of human action. As we argued in Chapter 3, God cannot otherwise intervene in human affairs without abrogating the autonomy of the created universe.

Christian communities in general, whether or not they fit the description of the new kinds of communities we describe above, should take on board the inescapable fact of religious plurality and the consequent difficulty of asserting with any confidence that specifically Christian claims are actually true. The church in all its versions must also acknowledge, without the least embarrassment or fear, that the external challenge of religious plurality is matched by an equally great if more internal challenge, namely, the challenge of establishing with confidence what actually occurred in the events recorded in its ancient, ambiguous, and controversial scriptures. We say the church should do so without fear because, once again, if it takes seriously certain commandments of its master that most scholars regard as among the best established, it should act at all times and in all matters in freedom from fear. Above all, the church should never fear the truth, because its very existence only matters if the truth is what it teaches.

A church of whatever size or structure that responds forthrightly to the kinds of concerns addressed in this book will openly acknowledge the legitimate presence of doubters and seekers, not just at the margins but at the center of its religious life. But at the same time, it will not shy away from affirming the reality and goodness of God, the holiness of God's creation, or the hope of fulfillment for those whose lives are blighted by the ravages of nature or of other human beings. And it will continue to offer—as an object of belief for some, a hoped-for possibility for others—the bold but at the same time modest offer of a connection to the one who, it proclaims, made present among us the infinite grace and compassion of the ultimate reality itself.

Notes

PREFACE

1. Among the positive examples we think in particular of Keith Ward, *Re-Thinking Christianity* (Oxford: One-World, 2007); John Cobb, Jr., *Reclaiming the Church* (Louisville, KY: Westminster John Knox Press, 1997); Elizabeth A. Johnson, *She Who Is: The Mystery of God in Feminist Theological Discourse* (New York: Crossroad, 1992); Catherine Keller, *Face of the Deep: A Theology of Becoming* (London: Routledge, 2003); Brian D. McLaren, e.g. *Everything Must Change: Jesus, Global Crises, and a Revolution of Hope* (Nashville, TN: Thomas Nelson, 2007) and *A New Kind of Christianity: Ten Questions that are Transforming the Faith* (New York, NY: HarperOne, 2010); Kathryn Tanner, *The Politics of God: Christian Theologies and Social Justice* (Minneapolis: Fortress Press, 1992) and *Jesus, Humanity and the Trinity: A Brief Systematic Theology* (Minneapolis: Fortress Press, 2001).

CHAPTER I

1. Whether we are now in a modern or "postmodern" context, and to what extent that changes discussions about ultimacy, is presently a matter of heated discussion. The debate over the last quarter century was fueled by Jean-François Lyotard's book, *The Postmodern Condition: A Report on Knowledge* (Minneapolis: University of Minnesota Press, 1984).

2. Although dozens could be listed, a particularly clear example of this strategy is John Shelby Spong, *Why Christianity Must Change or Die: A Bishop Speaks to Believers in Exile* (San Francisco, CA: HarperSanFrancisco, 1998). For a more nuanced rethinking of Christianity for the modern context, see the publications by Marcus J. Borg; we recommend in particular *The Heart of Christianity: Rediscovering a Life of Faith* (San Francisco: HarperSanFrancisco, 2003). Multiple proposals from Jesus Seminar participants are collected in *The Once and Future Jesus* (Santa Rosa, CA: Polebridge Press, 2000). Mark C. Taylor reinterprets Christian belief for one important form of postmodernity, poststructuralism, in *Erring: A Postmodern A/theology* (Chicago: University of Chicago Press, 1984). Many of these efforts go back to the pioneering work of the mid-twentieth-century German theologian Rudolf Bultmann, who sought to present a

"demythologized," purely existential version of Christianity; see e.g. his *Faith and Understanding*, ed. Robert W. Funk (Philadelphia: Fortress Press, 1987) and *Existence and Faith: Shorter Writings of Rudolf Bultmann*, trans. Schubert M. Ogden (New York: World Publishing, 1960). We stand closer to Paul Tillich than to Bultmann, insofar as Tillich described ways of believing differently, even in the face of doubt, rather than demythologizing Christianity and then believing what was left over. Accessible works by Tillich include *The Courage to Be*, 2nd ed. (New Haven: Yale University Press, [1952], 2000) and *Dynamics of Faith* (New York: HarperPerennial, [1957], 2001).

3. A thoughtful version of this approach is that of Diogenes Allen; see e.g. *Three Outsiders: Pascal, Kierkegaard, Simone Weil* (Cambridge, MA: Cowley Publications, 1983) and *Christian Belief in a Postmodern World: The Full Wealth of Conviction* (Louisville, KY: Westminster John Knox Press, 1989). Note that we are not suggesting that human reason can comprehend the divine reality itself.

4. Classic representatives of this approach include David Tracy (see *The Analogical Imagination: Christian Theology and the Culture of Pluralism* [New York: Crossroad, 1981] and *Plurality and Ambiguity: Hermeneutics, Religion, Hope* [San Francisco: Harper & Row, 1987]) and Paul Ricoeur (*The Symbolism of Evil* [New York: Harper & Row, 1967]; *Essays on Biblical Interpretation*, ed. Lewis S. Mudge [Philadelphia: Fortress Press, 1980]; *Figuring the Sacred: Religion, Narrative, and Imagination* [Minneapolis: Fortress Press, 1995]).

5. Hans Albert popularized the phrase "immunization strategy" in *Treatise on Critical Reason* (Princeton: Princeton University Press, 1985). The inspiration for Albert's position comes from the emphasis on conclusive falsifications in the work of the great philosopher of science Karl Popper; see e.g. Popper, *Conjectures and Refutations: The Growth of Scientific Knowledge* (London: Routledge and Kegan Paul, 1969).

6. David Hume, *Of Miracles* (La Salle, IL: Open Court, 1985).

7. The problem of multiple religions is of course reproduced within Christianity as the problem of multiple communities, denominations, and sects. We return to the connections between these two topics in Chapter 8.

8. It is in one sense inaccurate to suggest that Christianity owes its existence to Judaism per se. Judaism as we now know it developed during the period of exile or diaspora that followed the Roman destruction of the Second Temple in 70 CE and that ended the system of sacrificial worship that had been a central feature of religion in ancient Judea. From that point of view, Judaism and Christianity were contemporaneous as well as conflicting responses to the Hebrew scriptures to which both laid claim. On the other hand, the most prominent of the earliest Christian writers, Paul, counted himself among "the Jews" even after his conversion, and regarded them, despite their rejection of Christian claims, as the proper and irreplaceable heirs of the ancient tradition (Romans 9–11).

9. See John Dominic Crossan's fine summary of the textual history in *The Historical Jesus: The Life of a Mediterranean Jewish Peasant* (San Francisco: Harper, 1991).

10. Among feminist biblical scholars, the work of Elisabeth Schüssler Fiorenza has had perhaps the greatest impact. See e.g. her excellent introduction, *Wisdom Ways: Introducing Feminist Biblical Interpretation* (Maryknoll, NY: Orbis Books, 2001), as well as *The Power of the Word: Scripture and the Rhetoric of Empire* (Minneapolis: Augsburg Fortress, 2007). Important feminist rereadings of the New Testament include Luise Schottroff, Silvia Schroer, and Marie-Theres Wacker, *Feminist Interpretation: The Bible in Women's Perspective* (Minneapolis: Fortress Press, 1998); Luise Schottroff, *The Parables of Jesus* (Minneapolis: Augsburg Fortress, 2006); Sandra Polaski, *A Feminist Introduction to Paul* (St. Louis: Chalice Press, 2005); and Sandra Polaski, *Paul and the Discourse of Power* (Sheffield: Sheffield Academic Press, 1999). Other works that have helped to "pluralize" the reading of the New Testament include Amy-Jill Levine, *The Misunderstood Jew: The Church and the Scandal of the Jewish Jesus* (New York: HarperCollins, 2006) and *An Essential Guide to the Jewish Context of the New Testament* (Nashville, TN: Abingdon Press, 2009); and, from a non-Western perspective, Kwok Pui-Lan, *Discovering the Bible in the Non-Biblical World* (Maryknoll, NY: Orbis Books, 1995) and *Christology for an Ecological Age* (New York: Continuum, 1999).

11. For an account of how these texts were unearthed, see Jean Doresse, *The Discovery of the Nag Hammadi Texts: A Firsthand Account of the Expedition that Shook the Foundations of Christianity* (Rochester, VT: Inner Traditions, 2005). The texts themselves can be found in *The Nag Hammadi Scriptures*, ed. Marvin Meyer (New York: HarperOne, 2007).

12. Study of the extensive literature in philosophy and theology on the topics of doubt and commitment confirms this impression. Full references to that literature and to our interpretation of its implications can be found in our technical publications. See Clayton, *Explanation from Physics to Theology: An Essay in Rationality and Religion* (New Haven: Yale University Press, 1989); Clayton, *God and Contemporary Science* (Edinburgh: Edinburgh University Press, and Grand Rapids, MI: Eerdmans, 1997); Clayton and Knapp, "Belief and the Logic of Religious Commitment," in Godehard Bruntrup and Ronald K. Tacelli, eds., *The Rationality of Religious Belief* (Dordrecht: Kluwer Academic Press, 1999), 61–83; Clayton and Knapp, "Is Holistic Justification Enough?" and "Rationality and Christian Self-Conceptions," in Mark Richardson and Wesley Wildman, eds., *Religion and Science: History, Method, Dialogue* (London: Routledge, 1996); Clayton and Knapp, "Rationality and Religious Self-Conceptions," *Bulletin of the Center for Theology and the Natural Sciences* 12/2 (1992): 9–15; Clayton, *Adventures in the Spirit: God, World, Divine Action* (Minneapolis: Fortress Press, 2008).

13. The phrase "Christian minimalism" was suggested by the late Bernard Williams in a conversation with one of the authors—which is not to suggest that he would have endorsed our arguments or conclusions. Only in the final phase of working on this book did we discover the intriguing concept of "minimal religion" advanced by Mikhail Epstein. Near the end of *A Secular Age* (Cambridge, MA: Belknap Press, 2007), Charles Taylor writes, "this heavy concentration of the atmosphere of immanence will intensify a sense of living in a 'waste land' for subsequent generations, and many young people will again begin to explore beyond these boundaries. Where this will lead, no one can predict, although, perhaps the intimations of Mikhail Epstein, which I described at the end of Chapter 14, may turn out to be prescient" (770). See the fascinating article by Epstein, "Minimal Religion," Chapter 12 of Mikhail Epstein, Alexander Genis, and Slobodanka Vladiv-Glover, *Russian Postmodernism: New Perspectives on Post-Soviet Culture* (Providence, RI: Berghahn Books, 1999), 163–71, and, in the same work, on "postatheism" also pp. 378–90. (We are grateful to Brian McLaren for this reference.) The post-Communist-era context in Russia today is vastly different from the American religious context, as is Epstein's minimal religion from our notion of Christian minimalism. The analogies are nonetheless intriguing.

14. See, among his many works on this topic, John Shelby Spong's *Jesus for the Non-Religious: Recovering the Divine at the Heart of the Human* (New York: HarperSanFrancisco, 2007). See also John Dominic Crossan's publications, such as *The Birth of Christianity: Discovering What Happened in the Years Immediately after the Execution of Jesus* (San Francisco: Harper SanFrancisco, 1998) and (with Jonathan L. Reed) *Excavating Jesus: Beneath the Stones, Behind the Texts* (San Francisco: HarperSanFrancisco, 2001). Gerd Lüdemann also qualifies as a maximal minimalist in works such as *The Resurrection of Christ: A Historical Inquiry* (Amherst, NY: Prometheus Books, 2004).

15. Josh McDowell, *The New Evidence that Demands a Verdict, Fully Updated to Answer the Questions Challenging Christians Today* (Nashville, TN: Thomas Nelson, 1999).

16. See Alvin Plantinga's trilogy of books on warrant: *Warrant: The Current Debate* (New York: Oxford University Press, 1993); *Warrant and Proper Function* (New York: Oxford University Press, 1993); and especially *Warranted Christian Belief* (New York: Oxford University Press, 2000).

CHAPTER 2

1. On "normal" science and the transitions from one normal science to another see Thomas S. Kuhn, *The Structure of Scientific Revolutions*, 3rd ed. (Chicago: University of Chicago Press, [1962], 1996).

2. See Daniel C. Dennett, *Darwin's Dangerous Idea: Evolution and the Meanings of Life* (New York: Simon & Schuster, 1995).

3. Richard Dawkins, *The God Delusion* (Boston: Houghton Mifflin, 2006).

4. Quoted from Edward Lear, *Queery Leary Nonsense: A Lear Nonsense Book*, ed. Lady [Constance] Strachey (London: Mills & Boon, 1911).

5. See e.g. Franz M. Wuketits and Francisco J. Ayala, eds., *Handbook of Evolution*, 3 vols. (Weinheim: Wiley-VCH, 2004). For a briefer introduction, see Niles Eldridge, *The Pattern of Evolution* (New York: W. H. Freeman, 1999); or Stephen Jay Gould, *Wonderful Life: The Burgess Shale and the Nature of History* (New York: W. W. Norton, 1989); or, more recently Edward J. Larson, *Evolution: The Remarkable History of a Scientific Theory* (New York: Modern Library, 2006).

6. The classic work on the "coevolution" of biology and culture is William H. Durham, *Coevolution: Genes, Culture, and Human Diversity* (Stanford, CA: Stanford University Press, 1991); see also Philip Clayton, *In Quest of Freedom: The Emergence of Spirit in the Natural World* (Göttingen: Vandenhoeck & Ruprecht, 2009). On evolutionary psychology see David M. Buss, ed., *The Handbook of Evolutionary Psychology* (Hoboken, NJ: John Wiley & Sons, 2005).

7. The genesis of each thing "according to its kind" was a core assumption in Greek philosophy. Even René Descartes, the so-called father of modern philosophy, still assumed in his *Meditations* that the cause of any phenomenon had to contain at least as much reality as the effect itself. See René Descartes, *Meditations on First Philosophy*, trans. Michael Moriarty (Oxford: Oxford University Press, 2008).

8. Indeed, it's typically the *opponents* of emergence theory who argue that "like must stem from like." For example, panpsychists hold that if some sort of subjective experience (mind or consciousness) was not present as a quality of things in this world from the very beginning, it could not have emerged over the course of evolutionary history. But emergence theorists deny this premise; they maintain that even qualities radically different from physical and chemical properties—properties such as minds and intentions, purpose and value—can arise as a part of the evolution of complexity. This explains why we argue in the text that apologists are wrong to argue directly from the emergence of mental properties in this universe to the existence of a personal God.

9. The classic text is John D. Barrow and Frank J. Tipler, *The Anthropic Cosmological Principle* (Oxford: Oxford University Press, 1986).

10. The alleged implications for the existence of God are worked out in Michael Anthony Corey, *God and the New Cosmology: The Anthropic Design Argument* (Savage, MD: Rowman & Littlefield, 1993) or (in our view rather overambitiously) in Hugh Ross, *The Creator and the Cosmos: How the Greatest Scientific Discoveries of the Century Reveal God*, 3rd ed. (Colorado Springs, CO: NavPress, 2001). Critics include Paul Davies,

Cosmic Jackpot: Why Our Universe is Just Right for Life (Boston: Houghton Mifflin, 2007) and Nick Bostrom, *Anthropic Bias: Observation Selection Effects in Science and Philosophy* (New York: Routledge, 2002).

11. The so-called Intelligent Design movement uses a form of the traditional anthropic argument but adds the claim that specific examples of order in the universe *could not be explained* without the hypothesis of God qua intelligent Designer. See for example Michael J. Behe, *Darwin's Black Box: The Biochemical Challenge to Evolution* (New York: Free Press, 1996); William A. Dembski, *The Design Inference: Eliminating Chance through Small Probabilities* (Cambridge: Cambridge University Press, 1998) and Dembski, "In Defense of Intelligent Design," in Philip Clayton, ed., *The Oxford Handbook of Religion and Science* (Oxford: Oxford University Press, 2006), 715–31.

12. We recommend in particular Del Ratzsch, *Nature, Design, and Science: The Status of Design in Natural Science* (Albany, NY: State University of New York Press, 2001) and Ratzsch, *The Battle of Beginnings: Why Neither Side is Winning the Creation–Evolution Debate* (Downers Grove, IL: Inter-Varsity Press, 1996). Among a number of books that are sharply critical of the Intelligent Design movement, see Robert T. Pennock, *Tower of Babel: The Evidence against the New Creationism* (Cambridge, MA: MIT Press, 1999).

13. On the more recent debate see Bernard Carr, ed., *Universe or Multiverse?* (Cambridge: Cambridge University Press, 2007). Rodney D. Holder derives theistic conclusions in *God, the Multiverse, and Everything: Modern Cosmology and the Argument from Design* (Aldershot, UK, and Burlington, VT: Ashgate, 2004), and Paul Davies challenges these conclusions in *Cosmic Jackpot*.

14. These postulations across universes are mathematical and highly technical. The best recent popular presentation in which nonspecialists can gain a sense of how these postulations work, and why they are necessary, is Alexander Vilenkin, *Many Worlds in One: The Search for Other Universes* (New York: Hill and Wang, 2006). The astrophysicist George Ellis has challenged the scientific status of multiverse theory on purely scientific grounds; see e.g. George Ellis, "Physics Ain't What It Used To Be," *Nature* 438 (2005): 739–40; online at www.nature.com/nature/journal/v438/n7069/full/438739a.html (accessed May 7, 2011).

15. Although this insight was classically described as the discovery of a mental dimension of reality, as in Plato's theory of the forms, strictly speaking it involves three different types of reality. Beyond the world of physical things one must postulate a "world" of logical and mathematical truths and a "world" of the Mind or minds that know them. Karl Popper formulated this "three worlds" position some decades back; it was later reformulated and defended by the Oxford mathematical physicist Roger Penrose; see e.g. *Shadows of the Mind: A Search for the Missing Science of*

Consciousness (Oxford: Oxford University Press, 1994). Penrose argues, for example, that "Ideas that were developed for the sole purpose of deepening our understanding of the physical world have very frequently provided profound and unexpected insights into mathematical problems that had already been objects of considerable interest for quite separate reasons. One the most striking recent examples of this was the use of Yang–Mills-Type Theories by Oxford's Simon Donaldson, to obtain totally unexpected properties of four-dimensional manifolds—properties that had eluded understanding for many years previously" (416). It is wrongly argued that respect for science requires one to acknowledge only the physical world and deny ontological status to the others. In fact, this and other examples show that the success of science is better explained by an ontology of three "worlds" than only one.

16. See Michael F. Wagner, ed., *Neoplatonism and Nature: Studies in Plotinus' Enneads* (Albany, NY: State University of New York Press, 2002) or, at a more accessible level, Kevin Corrigan, *Reading Plotinus: A Practical Introduction to Neoplatonism* (West Lafayette, IN: Purdue University Press, 2005).

17. David Hume, *Dialogues Concerning Natural Religion* (Indianapolis: Bobbs-Merrill, 1970).

18. The account of reality we refer to is the "three worlds ontology" described in note 15 above.

19. John Hick's *An Interpretation of Religion* (New Haven: Yale University Press, 1989) remains a classic manifesto for this view. The position receives a sophisticated defense in Robert C. Neville's publications, e.g., *Creativity and God: A Challenge to Process Theology* (New York: Seabury Press, 1980) and *Behind the Masks of God: An Essay toward Comparative Theology* (Albany, NY: State University of New York Press, 1991). Neville's student Wesley J. Wildman is now advancing a similar research program in the philosophy of religion; see e.g. *Science and Religious Anthropology: A Spiritually Evocative Naturalist Interpretation of Human Life* (Burlington, VT: Ashgate, 2009).

20. Friedrich Wilhelm Joseph von Schelling, *Philosophical Inquiries into the Nature of Human Freedom* (La Salle, IL: Open Court, 1936); Alfred North Whitehead, *Process and Reality: An Essay in Cosmology*, corrected ed. (New York: Free Press, 1978).

21. See Charles Hartshorne and William L. Reese, eds., *Philosophers Speak of God* (Amherst, NY: Humanity Books, 2000).

22. See John Polkinghorne, ed., *The Work of Love: Creation as Kenosis* (Grand Rapids, MI: Eerdmans, 2001); Philip Clayton, *Adventures in the Spirit: God, World, Divine Action* (Minneapolis: Fortress Press, 2008).

23. Of course there are still darker possibilities: for instance, that the UR created our universe not just for some amoral purpose but for a positively evil one, such as enjoying the suffering of beings weaker than itself. While

it would take a much longer argument to show why such speculations are problematic, one problem is that they lead, sooner or later, to massively skeptical implications for the very possibility of finite rational agency. After all, if we suppose that the creative power behind the universe is not only indifferent but positively hostile to our welfare, we lose, among other things, any reason to suppose that our efforts to understand the universe have any chance of succeeding. In that sense, an attempt to argue that the UR is actually evil turns out to be self-defeating.

24. This idea that the highest form of existence the UR could enjoy would be self-contemplation goes back to the last chapters of Aristotle's *Nicomachean Ethics*, where he characterizes the UR as *nous noetikos,* thought thinking itself. There is even more richness and variety in the UR if it consists of multiple aspects or agents or persons, as is maintained, for example, in Trinitarian forms of belief in God.

25. See Anders Nygren, *Agape and Eros* (London: SPCK, 1953).

26. These results naturally give rise to reflections on the relation between values and community. Above we found reason to attribute to the UR not only something like mind but also values. We have further suggested in note 23 above that it is self-defeating to posit that these values are fundamentally opposed to the most basic values manifested in, or presupposed by, human agency. A nuanced position has begun to emerge on how the values that characterize the UR will be unlike, but in certain specific respects also similar to, human values. But so far we have not addressed, except in passing, the undeniable fact that human values develop and exist in the context of human community. Because this line of thought is rather more speculative than the arguments given in the main text, we present it here in the notes:

In the first place, of course, human beings only acquire whatever values they end up acquiring through their exposure to the norms of the interpersonal communities into which they are born, as well as the norms of whatever communities they may later join. The process, which social scientists as well as philosophers have analyzed in rich detail, usually begins with the communities constituted by each individual's immediate family, but it *always* begins, and begins necessarily, with what the individual learns from interacting with other persons.

Communities are not only, however, the original source of one's values. They also satisfy a necessary condition of pursuing those values once one has them, at least if one wants to do so in a rational way. It is only through ongoing interaction with a relevant community of other persons that an individual human being can receive the feedback she needs to ensure that her actions are consistent with the implications of the values she has derived from that community. For any individual human agent, having and pursuing values of whatever kind (aesthetic or economic values just as much as moral ones) requires participation in a community or series of communities from which the agent can derive not only the content of her values but ongoing feedback about how those values ought to be defined, refined, and realized, whether in the agent's day-to-day actions or in her larger projects. Indeed, without such feedback, rational agents have no way of developing or maintaining the self-conceptions in terms of which their goals and projects can make sense in the first place—even to themselves!

We have argued elsewhere that the need to obtain feedback from other persons imposes a certain minimal degree of altruism on all rational agents, including those whose ultimate aims are far from altruistic. It turns out, for example, that even the most minimal account of the ethical entailments of rational agency include the requirement of truthfulness. (See Philip Clayton and Steven Knapp, "Ethics and Rationality," *American Philosophical Quarterly* 30 [1993]: 151–61.)

In short, the development and pursuit of human values, no matter of what kind, are inseparable from participation in an axiological community. Such participation may take the form of engaging in public discussion or merely of registering nonverbal clues. In any case, it seems clear that a human being can only pursue the values that matter to her if she is open, at least in some degree, to the guidance of others.

How, then, might the kind of infinite being described in the previous section—a UR characterized by the selfless love of others—respond to the need of its rational creatures for axiological guidance? It seems reasonable to suppose that a UR correctly conceived in such terms would be disposed to help provide such guidance itself, assuming it was possible for the UR to do so. A divine agent conceived in these terms would be disposed not only to guide us in the understanding and pursuit of our particular values but also to guide us toward the pursuit of the kinds of values that would be most conducive to our flourishing. In that sense, it seems reasonable to suppose that the UR would become a member— indeed, perhaps the most important member—of our axiological community. And what about the UR itself as an axiological agent? Does the UR also need a community through which it can form and sustain its own values, and its own axiological self-conception? We have already suggested that the UR, as the infinite source of all that is, cannot be regarded as *needing* to be completed by the existence of anyone or anything outside itself. In that sense, the UR is necessarily free of the dependence on others that, we assert, is a necessary component of all human agency. On the other hand, it is possible to argue that not only an agent's self-conception but even her very existence as a person is inconceivable apart from her relation to other persons. See Michael Theunissen, *The Other: Studies in the Social Ontology of Husserl, Heidegger, Sartre, and Buber*, trans. C. Macann (Cambridge, MA: MIT Press, 1986), and most famously the various publications by Charles Taylor, e.g., *Sources of the Self: The Making of the Modern Identity* (Cambridge, MA: Harvard University Press, 1989); *Human Agency and Language* (New York: Cambridge University Press, 1985); and *The Ethics of Authenticity* (Cambridge, MA: Harvard University Press, 1992). If such arguments are correct, and if we are right in asserting that the UR is necessarily independent of anyone or anything outside itself, then it would follow that attributing to the UR values—and therefore personhood—of any kind involves the assumption that the UR must contain within itself what is already a community of persons. Clearly, to be drawn in this direction is to be drawn in the direction of Trinitarian conceptions of the divine, a topic to which we return in Chapters 6 and 7.

27. See Peter Berger, *A Rumor of Angels* (Harmondsworth, UK: Penguin Books, 1971). He writes, "By signals of transcendence I mean phenomena that are to be found within the domain of our 'natural' reality but that appear to point beyond that reality. In other words, I am not using transcendence here in a technical philosophical sense but, literally, as the transcending of the normal, everyday world that I earlier identified with the notion of the 'supernatural'" (70).

28. Actually, theists over the centuries and across the traditions have taken very different positions on whether God needs to exist in relationship to a world. Christian theologians have most often argued that the creation of the world is an act of divine grace and an expression of divine freedom, and this is possible only if God was not compelled to create. Still, Thomas Aquinas, deeply influenced by Aristotle, famously held open the possibility that the world is eternal, requiring only that its existence be contingent so that God alone exists necessarily. In the twentieth century, process theologians, following Alfred North Whitehead, have argued that God must always be accompanied by a world. See John B. Cobb, Jr., and David Ray Griffin, *Process Theology: An Introductory Exposition* (Philadelphia: Westminster Press, 1976).

CHAPTER 3

1. The quotation is taken from Wesley J. Wildman, "A Review and Critique of the 'Divine Action Project': A Dialogue among Scientists and Theologians, Sponsored by Pope John Paul II," unpublished MS, p. 3, and is used with permission. Published presentations of Wildman's views on these questions include his "The Divine Action Project, 1988–2003," *Theology and Science* 2 (2004): 31–75. Wildman's mature position is now available in *Science and Religious Anthropology: A Spiritually Evocative Naturalist Interpretation of Human Life* (Burlington, VT: Ashgate, 2009) and *Religious Philosophy as Multidisciplinary Comparative Inquiry: Envisioning a Future for the Philosophy of Religion* (Albany, NY: State University of New York Press, 2010).

2. As an example of this approach see Alvin Plantinga, "The Free Will Defense," in Baruch A. Brody, ed., *Readings in the Philosophy of Religion: An Analytic Approach*, 2nd ed. (Engelwood Cliffs, NJ: Prentice-Hall, 1992), 292–304.

3. At this general level, our hypothesis resembles what John Hick has called the "Iranaean" theodicy, which explains divine nonaction in terms of the conditions required for "soul-making," that is, for the formation and moral development of finite persons; see Hick, *Evil and the God of Love* (New York: Harper & Row, 1978).

4. Although some will be inclined to accept a libertarian account of human agency, the argument in this chapter does not presuppose it; a compatibilist should be able to endorse our thesis as well. For more on theories of agency that split the difference between libertarian and compatibilist arguments, see Philip Clayton, *In Quest of Freedom: The Emergence of Spirit in the Natural World*, Frankfurt Templeton Lectures 2006, ed. Michael G. Parker and Thomas M. Schmidt (Göttingen: Vandenhoeck & Ruprecht, 2009). We are concerned here with the minimal conditions for finite agency, that is, the conditions that must be met for finite agents to carry out actions with relative autonomy.

5. Cf. Charles S. Peirce, "The Fixation of Belief," first published in *Popular Science Monthly* 12 (Nov. 1877): 1–15, now in Nathan Houser and Christian Kloesel, eds., *The Essential Peirce: Selected Philosophical Writings*, vol. 1: *1867–1893* (Bloomington: Indiana University Press, 1992), 109–23.

6. Peirce thought that feedback from the relevant communities of inquiry was equally crucial to, and appropriate for, matters of religious concern: "if religious life is to ameliorate the world, it must... hold an abiding respect for truth. Such respect involves an openness to growth, to development. Thus, as ideas develop through the community of inquirers, they will have a gradual effect on religious belief and subsequently on religious practices." See Charles Hartshorne and Paul Weiss, eds., *The Collected Papers of Charles Sanders Peirce*, 8 vols. (Cambridge, MA: Harvard University Press, 1931–58), 1:184.

7. The example is taken from Alvin Plantinga, *God, Freedom, and Evil* (New York: Harper & Row, 1974).

8. Cf. George Eliot's famous comment in *Middlemarch* (London: Penguin Classics, [1871–2], 1994), chapter 20: "we do not expect people to be deeply moved by what is not unusual. That element of tragedy which lies in the very fact of frequency, has not yet wrought itself into the coarse emotion of mankind; and perhaps our frames could hardly bear much of it. If we had a keen vision and feeling of all ordinary human life, it would be like hearing the grass grow and the squirrel's heart beat, and we should die of that roar which lies on the other side of silence. As it is, the quickest of us walk about well wadded with stupidity."

9. Nancey Murphy has helpfully formulated the objection in this way in correspondence.

10. The philosopher Donald Davidson is perhaps the most famous advocate of anomalous monism. See e.g. Davidson, "Mental Events," reprinted in *Essays on Actions and Events* (Oxford: Clarendon Press, 1980), 207–24.

11. Donald Davidson, "The Irreducibility of Psychological and Physiological Description, and of Social to Physical Sciences," in Leslie Stevenson, ed., *The Study of Human Nature* (Oxford: Oxford University Press, 1981), 321.

12. By contrast, we have every reason to accept the existence of laws in physics, and at least some biologists support the existence of "general laws" of biology. See Stuart A. Kauffman, *Investigations* (Oxford: Oxford University Press, 2000).

13. The reasons for the failure of the reductivist program have been described by many philosophers. See e.g. Stuart Kauffman and Philip Clayton, "On Emergence, Agency, and Organization," *Philosophy and Biology* 21 (2006): 501–21.

14. Philosophers of mind have argued that the properties of the mental are different enough from physical properties that the two cannot be identified as instances of a single type of property. Among the qualities of mental events, it appears, are their "first-personal" or subjective character, their intentional and hence teleological structure, and their nonnomological nature. This difference is more accurately expressed, however, by the phrase "property emergentism" than the phrase "property dualism." The latter suggests that there is one and only one fundamental ontological divide in the natural world, that between mental and physical phenomena. (This seems to be the view of, for example, William Hasker in *The Emergent Self* [Ithaca: Cornell University Press, 1999].) By contrast, recent studies of emergent phenomena in science and the philosophy of science show that multiple levels of emergence are manifested across natural history. If in addition to the mental many other levels of distinct properties exist in the natural world, "dualism" is not an accurate label for this position.

15. Davidson's materialism compelled him to accept epiphenomenalism, the view that the mental is without causal efficacy in the world. It is not clear to us, however, that either scientific or philosophical arguments require one to accept this conclusion. Jaegwon Kim has argued for the dilemma, "either epiphenomenalism or the rejection of the causal closure of the physical world" (Kim, "Making Sense of Emergence," *Philosophical Studies* 95 [1999]: 3–36). At a conference in Granada, Spain, some years ago, David Chalmers responded that the problem of consciousness requires one to select one of three major options: epiphenomenalism, dualism, or panpsychism. (The conference results have been published in Philip Clayton and Paul Davies, eds., *The Re-emergence of Emergence: The Emergentist Hypothesis from Science to Religion* [Oxford: Oxford University Press,

2006].) Since by "dualism" Chalmers presumably meant, minimally, denying the causal closure of the physical world, his trilemma naturally supplements Kim's dilemma.

16. Stuart A. Kauffman, *Investigations* (Oxford: Oxford University Press, 2000).

17. Distinctive properties emerge at many different levels in the process of explaining the natural world. It is not possible to explain the behavior of intentional human agents, nor presumably that of other complex organisms, as manifestations of underlying "covering laws"; Hempel's deductive–nomological or "DN" model for explanation is simply not relevant to scientific practice at these levels. But CCP was alleged to be necessary at all levels of explanation precisely in order that DN explanations would be possible. Drop the DN requirement on explanations, and the main argument for CCP disappears.

18. See e.g. Nancey Murphy, "Emergence and Mental Causation," in Clayton and Davies, eds., *The Re-emergence of Emergence*, 227–43. Such environmental factors are obscured in the standard diagrams, which show a specific idea or mental state M influencing a given bodily state B. M-predicates are a highly complex type of property; they cannot be defined only with reference to a single body and the neurophysiological processes that produce a particular instance or "token" mental state.

19. The roots of this theory of "embedded mind" go back to the early work of Humberto Maturana and Francisco Varela; see their *The Tree of Knowledge: The Biological Roots of Human Understanding*, rev. ed., trans. Robert Paolucci (New York: Random House, 1992).

20. Referring to a person's mental states and the various cultural and intellectual influences upon them is part of explaining the physical state of her body. Such factors can be included only if explanations are given in terms of type–type influences rather than in the (to us conceptually problematic) language of "this idea" influencing "that brain state." Presumably this conclusion is true not only for persons but for any entities that manifest holistic properties as complex as mental properties.

21. Different scholars give somewhat different accounts of this relationship. For panentheists, for example—those who locate all created reality within God—spiritual qualities are already in some sense divine properties. This move makes it even more natural to speak of a divine as well as a human element in the evolution of these properties.

22. William James, *Varieties of Religious Experience: A Study in Human Nature* (London and New York: Routledge, 2002).

23. Of course, if the agent takes on this general value, it will become part of her pattern of agency and will presumably affect others of her actions as well.

24. The best-known defenses of revelation as a series of "divine speech acts" are Nicholas Wolterstorff, *Divine Discourse: Philosophical Reflections on the Claim that God Speaks* (Cambridge: Cambridge University Press, 1995), and Kevin J. Vanhoozer, *The Drama of Doctrine: A Canonical-Linguistic Approach to Christian Theology* (Louisville, KY: Westminster John Knox Press, 2005).

25. This latter view has been widely endorsed by liberal theologians since the famous Chicago School philosophical theologian Henry Nelson Wieman. Advocates include Gordon D. Kaufman (*In the Beginning—Creativity* [Minneapolis: Fortress Press, 2004]); Karl E. Peters (*Dancing with the Sacred: Evolution, Ecology, and God* [Harrisburg, PA: Trinity Press International, 2002]); and more recently Stuart A. Kauffman (*Reinventing the Sacred: A New View of Science, Reason and Religion* [New York: Basic Academic, 2008]).

26. See Philip Clayton, *Mind and Emergence: From Quantum to Consciousness* (Oxford: Oxford University Press, 2004); Clayton and Davies, eds., *The Re-emergence of Emergence;* Nancey Murphy and William R. Stoeger, SJ, eds., *Evolution and Emergence: Systems, Organisms, Persons* (Oxford: Oxford University Press, 2007).

27. The *Oxford Dictionary of the Christian Church* defines panentheism as "the belief that the Being of God includes and penetrates the whole universe, so that every part of it exists in Him, but (as against Pantheism) that His Being is more than, and is not exhausted by, the universe." See Philip Clayton and Arthur Peacocke, eds., *In Whom We Live and Move and Have Our Being: Panentheistic Reflections on God's Presence in a Scientific World* (Grand Rapids, MI: Eerdmans, 2004); John Cooper, *Panentheism, the Other God of the Philosophers: From Plato to the Present* (Grand Rapids, MI: Baker Academic, 2006).

28. For more detail, see Clayton, *In Quest of Freedom*, and *Adventures in the Spirit: God, World, Divine Action* (Minneapolis: Fortress Press, 2008).

29. Fyodor Dostoevsky, *The Brothers Karamazov*, trans. R. Pevear and L. Volokhonsky (New York: Knopf, 1992), ch. 4. This is the text that immediately precedes the story of the Grand Inquisitor in ch. 5.

30. Note that the emergentist theory of mind developed above coheres with and at least indirectly supports this processual understanding of the divine creative intent.

31. Hick develops his "soul-making" theodicy in *Evil and the God of Love* (note 3 above).

CHAPTER 4

1. This is the view often known as pantheism; see Michael P. Levine, *Pantheism: A Non-theistic Concept of Deity* (London: Routledge, 2003).

2. Of course, there are a variety of religions that do not involve a reference to an ultimate reality; their concern with ultimacy, if it is thematized at all, is a concern with one's final ethical, familial, or political duties; one's responsibilities to one's tribe or ancestors; or one's proper place in nature. Confucianism, Shintoism, and animistic religions are often placed in this category. Although this categorization is standard, it is not uncontroversial. For a good indication of the actual complexity, see the three volumes of published results from Boston University's "ultimate reality research project," each edited by Robert Cummings Neville and published by SUNY Press in 2001: *Religious Truth, Ultimate Realities,* and *The Human Condition.*

3. See e.g. Andrew Schoedinger, ed., *Introduction to Metaphysics: The Fundamental Questions* (Buffalo, NY: Prometheus Books, 1991); Michael J. Loux, ed., *Metaphysics: Contemporary Readings* (London and New York: Routledge, 2001); Michael J. Loux and Dean W. Zimmerman, eds., *The Oxford Handbook of Metaphysics* (Oxford: Oxford University Press, 2003); Peter van Inwagen and Dean W. Zimmerman, eds., *Metaphysics: The Big Questions,* 2nd ed. (Oxford: Blackwell, 2008).

4. See e.g. Pim Valkenberg, *Sharing Lights on the Way to God: Muslim–Christian Dialogue and Theology in the Context of Abrahamic Partnership* (Amsterdam: Rodopi, 2006).

5. See David F. Ford and C. C. Pecknold, eds., *The Promise of Scriptural Reasoning* (Oxford: Blackwell, 2006); Peter Ochs, ed., *The Return to Scripture in Judaism and Christianity: Essays in Postcritical Scriptural Interpretation* (New York: Paulist Press, 1993); John Howard Yoder, *The Jewish–Christian Schism Revisited,* ed. Michael G. Cartwright and Peter Ochs (Grand Rapids, MI: Eerdmans, 2003).

6. See Jürgen Moltmann's creative appropriation of Kabbalistic categories such as *zimzum* in his influential *God in Creation: An Ecological Doctrine of Creation* (London: SCM Press, 1985).

7. As we noted in Chapter 1, relations between Judaism and Christianity have been especially fraught, given the original emergence of Christianity in first-century Judaism, Jewish rejection of the earliest Christian claims, and the subsequent history of Christian recrimination, discrimination, and outright atrocities against Jewish communities. We will take up the general question of how Christian communities might more appropriately interact with non-Christian religious communities in Chapter 8.

8. Samuel Johnson famously asked, "As to religion, have we heard all that a disciple of Confucius, that a Mohametan can say for himself?" (Boswell, *Life of Johnson,* ch. 32). The skeptically conservative point of Johnson's question, as the context makes clear, was that the impossibility of fairly evaluating the alternatives made it irrational to leave the religion into which one had been born.

9. John Hick, *An Interpretation of Religion* (New Haven: Yale University Press, 1989).

10. See e.g. Matthew Fox, *One River, Many Wells: Wisdom Springing from Global Faiths* (New York: Jeremy P. Tarcher/Penguin, 2004).

11. See Alvin Plantinga, "Ad Hick," *Faith and Philosophy* 14 (1997): 295–8; Plantinga, "Pluralism: A Defense of Religious Exclusivism," in K. Meeker and Philip Quinn, eds., *The Philosophical Challenge of Religious Diversity* (New York: Oxford University Press, 2000), 172–92; cf. David Basinger, *Religious Diversity: A Philosophical Assessment* (Burlington, VT: Ashgate, 2002).

12. See Richard Swinburne, *The Christian God* (Oxford: Clarendon, 1994); *Responsibility and Atonement* (New York: Oxford University Press, 1989); *Revelation: From Metaphor to Analogy* (Oxford: Oxford University Press, 1992). Cf. Alan G. Padgett, ed., *Reason and the Christian Religion: Essays in Honour of Richard Swinburne* (New York: Oxford University Press, 1994).

13. Rahner writes, "We might therefore put it as follows: the 'anonymous Christian' in our sense of the term is the pagan after the beginning of the Christian mission, who lives in the state of Christ's grace through faith, hope and love, yet who has no explicit knowledge of the fact that his life is orientated in grace-given salvation to Jesus Christ." (Karl Rahner, *Theological Investigations*, vol. 14 [London: Darton, Longman & Todd, 1976], 283.) An interesting interview with Rahner on this topic can be found at www.innerexplorations.com/chtheomortext/kr.htm (accessed May 7, 2011).

14. Bernard Williams has worked out the importance of a theory of error in various works: *Ethics and the Limits of Philosophy* (Cambridge, MA: Harvard University Press, 1985), ch. 3, e.g. 42f.; *Descartes: The Project of Pure Enquiry* (London: Routledge, 2005), 166–78; *In the Beginning was the Deed* (Princeton: Princeton University Press, 2005), ch. 1, e.g. 11.

15. David Ray Griffin has made this point nicely in his introduction to Griffin, ed., *Deep Religious Pluralism* (Louisville, KY: Westminster John Knox Press, 2005), criticizing John Hick in particular for an ostensibly democratic position on other religions that is in fact hegemonic. At the same time, one can't help but notice the paradoxical status of religious theories that make the impossibility of religious truth an essential part of the "truth" they claim to teach.

CHAPTER 5

1. Historical research has raised difficult questions about the central Christian claims. Among many that could be listed, we mention in particular John Dominic Crossan, *The Historical Jesus: The Life of a Mediterranean Jewish Peasant* (San Francisco: Harper, 1991); John Dominic Crossan, *The Birth of Christianity: Discovering What Happened in the Years Immediately after the Execution of Jesus* (San Francisco: HarperSanFrancisco, 1998); John Dominic Crossan and Jonathan L. Reed, *Excavating Jesus: Beneath the Stones, Behind the Texts* (San

Francisco: HarperSanFrancisco, 2001); Gerd Lüdemann, *The Resurrection of Christ: A Historical Inquiry* (Amherst, NY: Prometheus Books, 2004); Marcus J. Borg and John Dominic Crossan, *The Last Week: The Day-by-Day Account of Jesus' Final Week in Jerusalem* (San Francisco: HarperSan Francisco, 2006); and Robert W. Funk, ed., *The Gospel of Jesus According to the Jesus Seminar* (Santa Rosa, CA: Polebridge Press, 1999). See also the debate between John Dominic Crossan and N. T. Wright, *The Resurrection of Jesus: In Dialogue*, ed. Robert B. Stewart (Minneapolis: Fortress Press, 2006).

Among the recent defenses of more traditional claims, see Luke Timothy Johnson, *The Real Jesus: The Misguided Quest for the Historical Jesus and the Truth of the Traditional Gospels* (San Francisco: HarperSanFrancisco, 1996); Gary R. Habermas, *The Risen Jesus & Future Hope* (Lanham, MD: Rowman & Littlefield, 2003); Habermas and Anthony G. N. Flew, *Did Jesus Rise from the Dead? The Resurrection Debate*, ed. Terry L. Miethe (San Francisco: Harper & Row, 1987); Raymond E. Brown, *A Risen Christ in Eastertime: Essays on the Gospel Narratives of the Resurrection* (Collegeville, MN: Liturgical Press, 1991); Stewart, ed., *The Resurrection of Jesus: John Dominic Crossan and N. T. Wright in Dialogue.*

2. This and subsequent quotations are drawn from the New Revised Standard Version (NRSV).

3. The works of the New Testament exegete and bishop N. T. Wright provide one scholarly, readable, and immensely influential account of the traditional view. In working toward the conclusions defended in the text, we have spent as much time wrestling with the writings of Wright and his allies as we have with their critics, such as John Dominic Crossan and other members (and guests) of the Jesus Seminar. In fact, the Wright–Crossan dialogue is available in print; see Stewart, ed., *The Resurrection of Jesus: John Dominic Crossan and N. T. Wright in Dialogue.* Wright has published a large number of scholarly articles and books; see for example Craig A. Evans and N. T. Wright, *Jesus, the Final Days: What Really Happened*, ed. Troy A. Miller (Louisville, KY: Westminster John Knox Press, 2009); N. T. Wright, *The Original Jesus: The Life and Vision of a Revolutionary* (Grand Rapids, MI: Eerdmans, 1996); and especially N. T. Wright, *Jesus and the Victory of God* (Minneapolis: Fortress Press, 1996).

4. Sources on these so-called Gnostic gospels are given in Alan Jacobs, ed., *The Essential Gnostic Gospels: Including the Gospel of Thomas, the Gospel of Mary Magdalene* (London: Watkins, 2006). Elaine Pagels' work provides the best introduction to these documents; see e.g. her *The Gnostic Gospels* (New York: Random House, 1979); *Beyond Belief: The Secret Gospel of Thomas* (New York: Random House, 2003); and *Reading Judas: The Gospel of Judas and the Shaping of Christianity* (New York: Viking,

2007). See also John Dominic Crossan, *Four Other Gospels: Shadows on the Contours of Canon* (Sonoma, CA: Polebridge Press, 1992).

5. Thus John Shelby Spong writes in *Resurrection: Myth or Reality? A Bishop's Search for the Origins of Christianity* (San Francisco: HarperOne, 1994), "Above all, words must be recognized as symbolic pointers to truth, not objective containers of truth" (37). Spong tends to treat the resurrection narratives in the same way he treats the narratives about the virgin birth. He writes, "As I first studied the birth narratives, it was clear that no major scholar of any persuasion took them literally" (14). For Spong, to do otherwise is unthinkable: "how long could the educated folk of the twentieth century continue to be literal about such things as the conception that occurred for a couple when both were well beyond menopause, the visit of the angel Gabriel, a pregnancy without a male agent, an angelic choir that sang in the sky, a star that roamed through the heavens, shepherds that have no trouble finding a baby in a city crowded with people called for a special census, and a king named Herod who would rely on three men he never met before to bring him an intelligence report about a pretender to his throne who was said to have been born just six miles away? If the divinity of Jesus was attached to the literal details of the birth tradition, then it was a doomed concept" (18). For Spong, the resurrection story is midrash; "it was a way to think mythologically about dimensions of reality for which the language of time and space were simply not appropriate" (16).

6. In Paul's writings, this notion seems disconnected from any claim about a miraculous birth (as it is also in the Johannine tradition) and only vaguely, and perhaps only figuratively, linked to a notion of Jesus' preexistence (which *may* have played a more strongly literal role in John's thinking).

7. Thus the theologian Michael Welker writes, "In the midst of tensions between palpable encounters and appearances, theophanies and doubt, the witnesses 'see' the risen Christ 'not with eyes only.' They 'see' him in his speaking to them, in the breaking of the bread, in the greeting of peace, in his opening to them the Scriptures, in his sending them, and in other signs. They 'see' him in actual and symbolic actions which become ritual forms of the liturgy and life of the church. Not a resuscitated Jesus, but the *whole* Jesus Christ and his life in its *fullness* become present in the resurrection. For a naturalistic and scientist way of thinking, it is not easy to make sense of this presence of the whole fullness of a person and a life 'in the Spirit and in faith.'" (Welker, "The Addressee of Divine Sustenance, Rescue, and Elevation: Toward a Nonreductive Understanding of Human Personhood," in Malcolm Jeeves, ed., *From Cells to Souls—and Beyond: Changing Portraits of Human Nature* [Grand Rapids, MI: Eerdmans, 2004], 227f.)

8. See James D. G. Dunn and Scot McKnight, eds., *The Historical Jesus in Recent Research* (Winona Lake, IN: Eisenbrauns, 2005); Craig A. Evans, ed., *The Historical Jesus*, 4 vols. (London and New York: Routledge, 2004);

Gerd Theissen and Annette Merz, *The Historical Jesus: A Comprehensive Guide* (Minneapolis: Fortress Press, 1998); Crossan, *The Historical Jesus*; John Dominic Crossan, *Jesus: A Revolutionary Biography* (San Francisco: HarperSanFrancisco, 1994); Robert W. Funk, ed., *The Acts of Jesus: The Search for the Authentic Deeds of Jesus* (San Francisco: HarperSanFrancisco, 1998).

9. Feminist biblical scholars have helped to uncover the role of patriarchal ideologies in theology and biblical studies. See in particular Melissa Raphael, *Theology and Embodiment: The Post-patriarchal Reconstruction of Female Sacrality* (Sheffield: Sheffield Academic Press, 1996); Rebecca S. Chopp and Mark Lewis Taylor, eds., *Reconstructing Christian Theology* (Minneapolis: Fortress Press, 1994); Rebecca S. Chopp and Sheila Greeve Davaney, eds., *Horizons in Feminist Theology: Identity, Tradition, and Norms* (Minneapolis: Fortress Press, 1997); and Catherine Keller, Michael Nausner, and Mayra Rivera, eds., *Postcolonial Theologies: Divinity and Empire* (St. Louis, MO: Chalice Press, 2004). The term "rescripturings" is due to Pietro Boiani.

10. This position has some similarities with Karl Rahner's famous concept of the "anonymous Christian," quoted in Chapter 4, note 13. Other passages in Rahner's *Theological Investigations* that elaborate this position include vol. 6, pp. 390–7, and vol. 16, pp. 202, 218–19. It is one thing to locate the Spirit of Christ wherever kenotic love is exhibited or encouraged, as we do; it is quite another thing, however, to assert that there is salvation only through Christ.

CHAPTER 6

1. See Rudolf Bultmann, *Existence and Faith: Shorter Writings of Rudolf Bultmann*, trans. Schubert M. Ogden (New York: World Publishing, 1960); Bultmann, *Faith and Understanding*, ed. Robert W. Funk (Philadelphia: Fortress Press, 1987).

2. One might conceive this somewhat in the manner of Wolfhart Pannenberg's account of the resurrection in *Jesus—God and Man*, trans. Lewis Wilkins and Duane Priebe (London: SCM Press, [1968], 2002).

3. Wolfhart Pannenberg is famous for his assertion of the presence of the end of history in the life, death, and resurrection of Jesus; see *Jesus—God and Man*. He adapts to this purpose the grammatical term *prolepsis*, which describes sentences in which future events are referred to in the present as present (e.g., calling someone "the dead man" because he will die soon). The life and resurrection of Jesus really was "proleptic," he argues, because in it the final telos of history really became manifest in the present. Alister McGrath comments, "History, in all its totality, can only be understood when it is viewed from its endpoint. This point alone

provides the perspective from which the historical process can be seen in its totality, and thus properly understood.... The end of history is disclosed proleptically in the history of Jesus Christ. In other words, the end of history, which has yet to take place, has been disclosed in advance of the event in the person and work of Christ" (Alister E. McGrath, *Historical Theology: An Introduction to the History of Christian Thought* [Oxford: Blackwell, 1998], 303).

4. Gerd Lüdemann, *What Really Happened to Jesus: A Historical Approach to the Resurrection*, trans. John Bowden (Louisville, KY: Westminster John Knox Press, 1995); Gerd Lüdemann, *The Resurrection of Jesus: History, Experience, Theology*, trans. John Bowden (London: SCM Press, 1994); Gerd Lüdemann, *The Resurrection of Christ: A Historical Inquiry* (Amherst, NY: Prometheus Books, 2004).

5. See e.g. Janice Smith and Earl V. Dunn, "Ghosts: Their Appearance During Bereavement," *Canadian Family Physician* 23 (Oct. 1977): 121–2; Dewi Rees, *Death and Bereavement: The Psychological, Religious, and Cultural Interfaces*, 2nd ed. (London: Whurr, 2001). For example, "Newly bereaved patients often experience hallucinations—auditory, visual, olfactory—about the deceased person. These experiences can be frightening to the patient, who will usually not mention them to anyone. However, the hallucinations can be used as a positive part of helping the bereaved adjust to their new life" (Smith and Dunn, 121).

6. Again, Gerd Lüdemann (see note 4) defends a psychological explanation of the New Testament account of Jesus' post-mortem appearances—but with the crucial difference that he leaves out any role for a genuine nonphysical presence.

7. See e.g. Jeff Astley, David Brown, and Ann Loades, eds. *Christology: Key Readings in Christian Thought* (Louisville, KY: Westminster John Knox Press, 2009).

8. We will return to this problem of what it means to revise traditional claims in our concluding chapter.

9. There is a large literature in philosophical theology and analytic philosophy of religion on the difficulties that arise from the claim that a person could be both infinite and finite at the same time. An important source for these objections in the recent discussion is John Hick, ed., *The Myth of God Incarnate* (London: SCM Press, 1977). Responses to the objection that the claim is incoherent appear in Thomas P. Flint and Michael C. Rea, eds., *The Oxford Handbook of Philosophical Theology* (Oxford: Oxford University Press, 2008); see esp. Richard Cross's article on "The Incarnation." Other treatments of the incoherence objection include Kathryn Tanner, *Jesus, Humanity and the Trinity: A Brief Systematic Theology* (Minneapolis: Fortress Press, 2001); Brian Leftow, "A Timeless God Incarnate," in Stephen T. Davis, ed., *The Incarnation: An Interdisciplinary Symposium on the Incarnation of the Son of God* (Oxford: Oxford University Press, 2002); Oliver Crisp,

Divinity and Humanity: The Incarnation Reconsidered (Cambridge: Cambridge University Press, 2007); Richard Cross, *The Metaphysics of the Incarnation* (Oxford: Oxford University Press, 2002); Thomas Morris, "The Metaphysics of God Incarnate," in Michael Rea, ed., *Oxford Readings in Philosophical Theology* (Oxford: Oxford University Press, 2009), as well as Morris's book, *The Logic of God Incarnate* (Ithaca, NY: Cornell University Press, 1986); and Andrew Loke, "On the Coherence of the Incarnation: The Divine Preconscious Model," in *Neue Zeitschrift für Systematische Theologie und Religionsphilosophie* 51/1 (2009): 50–63.

10. Some Christians have difficulties feeling the force of this objection: surely, they reason, God can intervene in history in a special way when it concerns salvation, even to the point of setting aside natural regularities and the laws on which the created order is based. But in a philosophical defense of the faith, the justice and consistency of God's actions must also be shown; it is not a matter of course that God can act differentially in history. Hearing this, some will opt out of the project of theodicy, that is, of giving a philosophical defense of their faith. As we have affirmed since the opening chapter, this response always remains open to the Christian believer when the costs of inquiry seem too great. What does *not* remain viable is to claim philosophical proof for one's faith without addressing the philosophers' objections.

11. There is another version of this theory of eschatological inbreaking in which the overlap or intersection of worlds is not due to an alignment of human and divine wills but is brought about from the divine side alone. It takes this form, for example, among Reformed theologians who place the primary stress on divine predestination of events. Given the conclusions established in Chapter 3, it should be clear why we would resist the theory in that form.

CHAPTER 7

1. Because it involves an appeal to the perspective of an entire community of inquiry, we have associated this position with the epistemology of C. S. Peirce. For Peirce, however, agreement among the experts provided not just the best reason for saying that a given proposition was likely to be true; agreement at the "end of inquiry" became for Peirce a *definition* of truth. We reject that ultimately idealist definition on the realist assumption that even a final consensus, could it ever be achieved, might still be mistaken. For that reason, our position is Peircean in a modified sense.

   Nonetheless, it makes more sense than not to classify our position as Peircean. On our view, an agent is rational insofar as she wants to make sure that her thoughts and actions are guided by the best propositions. The best possible propositions are those that are true, that is, that correspond to the way things actually are. But we have no direct means of telling which propositions correspond to the way things actually are. So the second best propositions, so to speak, are those we have the least reason to doubt. According to Peirce, we have no practical way of distinguishing the propositions we have the least reason to doubt from those that are actually true, and this led him to define truth itself, mistakenly in our view, as the absence of doubt. We can agree with Peirce on the question of what is possible in practice, even if we resist his ontological conclusion.

2. See information released by the US National Digestive Diseases Information Clearinghouse of the National Institutes of Health (NIH), available at http://digestive.niddk.nih.gov/ddiseases/pubs/hpylori/ (accessed May 7, 2011).

3. In the past we defined this stance as "possibilism"; see especially Clayton and Knapp, "Belief and the Logic of Religious Commitment," in Godehard Bruntrup and Ronald K. Tacelli, eds., *The Rationality of Religious Belief* (Dordrecht: Kluwer Academic Press, 1999), 61–83. The present formulation presents, we believe, a more accurate and more defensible description of this particular—and perhaps widespread—epistemic state and the conditions under which it is justified.

4. Samuel Taylor Coleridge, *Biographia Literaria*, II, ed. James Engell and W. Jackson Bate, in *The Collected Works of Samuel Taylor Coleridge*, vol. 7 (Princeton: Princeton University Press, 1983), 6.

5. See Richard Dawkins, *The God Delusion* (Boston: Houghton Mifflin, 2006).

6. We also explored in some detail the relation of this christological claim to the notion that what the Spirit made present after Jesus' death was not just the definitive, unsurpassable authority of Jesus' "mind" but in some sense Jesus himself, albeit in a spiritual rather than a physically embodied form.

7. See Alvin Plantinga, *God, Freedom, and Evil* (New York: Harper & Row, 1974), 108–12. The program in philosophical theology inspired by this reformulation of Anselm's ontological argument is further spelled out, for example, in Thomas V. Morris, *Anselmian Explorations: Essays in Philosophical Theology* (Notre Dame, IN: University of Notre Dame Press, 1987).

8. See Wolfhart Pannenberg, *Jesus—God and Man*, trans. Lewis Wilkins and Duane Priebe (London: SCM Press, [1968], 2002); William Lane Craig, *Assessing the New Testament Evidence for the Historicity of the Resurrection of Jesus* (Lewiston, NY: E. Mellen Press, 1989); Josh McDowell, *The New Evidence that Demands a Verdict, Fully Updated to Answer the Questions Challenging Christians Today* (Nashville, TN: Thomas Nelson, 1999); David Baggett, ed., *Did the Resurrection Happen?: A Conversation with Gary Habermas and Antony Flew* (Downers Grove, IL: IVP Books, 2009); Ralph O. Muncaster, *What is the Proof for the Resurrection?* (Eugene, OR: Harvest House, 2000).

9. See C. S. Lewis, *Mere Christianity* (New York: Macmillan, 1960).

10. See Rudolf Otto, *The Idea of the Holy: An Inquiry into the Non-rational Factor in the Idea of the Divine and its Relation to the Rational*, trans. John Harvey (Oxford: Oxford University Press, 1973): "it grips or stirs the human mind.... The feeling of it may at times come sweeping like a gentle tide, pervading the mind with a tranquil mood of deepest worship. It may pass over into a more set and lasting attitude of the soul, continuing, as it were, thrillingly vibrant and resonant, until at last it dies away and the soul resumes its 'profane,' nonreligious mood of everyday experience" (12f.). Later Otto describes it as the experience of the "Wholly Other" (25).

11. Philosophers associate the concept of participation with the Platonic tradition. Plato affirmed the existence of a realm of ideal "forms," such as the form of justice or goodness. On this view, an act is just insofar as it exemplifies, or participates in, justice itself. Much subsequent philosophy and theology in the West bears the imprint of this framework. Gradually, the realm of the forms came to be associated with what was most real; an object was said to exist only insofar as it participated in the forms (or in God, in whom all exemplars dwell). Likewise, for someone to be good came to mean not just her exemplifying the form of goodness but, more generally, her prioritizing the realm of the divine exemplars over all worldly pursuits. For one theological appropriation see Samuel M. Powell, *Participating in God: Creation and Trinity* (Minneapolis: Fortress Press, 2003).

12. See Lewis S. Ford, *The Lure of God: A Biblical Background for Process Theism* (Philadelphia: Fortress Press, 1978).

13. See Philip Clayton and Arthur Peacocke, eds., *In Whom We Live and Move and Have Our Being: Panentheistic Reflections on God's Presence in a Scientific World* (Grand Rapids, MI: Eerdmans, 2004); Philip Clayton, *Adventures in the Spirit: God, World, Divine Action* (Minneapolis: Fortress Press, 2008); John Cooper, *Panentheism, the Other God of the Philosophers: From Plato to the Present* (Grand Rapids, MI: Baker Academic, 2006).

14. The roots of this idea go back to the Cappadocian Fathers in the fourth century CE, and theologies of this sort have been developed in their deepest form by the great theologians of the Eastern church. See Anthony Meredith, *The Cappadocians* (London: Geoffrey Chapman, 1995).

CHAPTER 8

1. *USA Today*, April 27, 2010, http://www.usatoday.com/news/religion/2010-04-27-1Amillfaith27_ST_N.htm (accessed May 7, 2011).

2. Philip Clayton, *Transforming Christian Theology* (Minneapolis: Fortress Press, 2009), 57–9.

3. Phyllis Tickle, *The Great Emergence: How Christianity is Changing and Why* (Grand Rapids, MI: Baker Academic, 2008).

4. Eddie Gibbs and Ryan K. Bolder, *Emerging Churches: Creating Christian Community in Postmodern Cultures* (Grand Rapids, MI: Baker Academic, 2005); Brian McLaren, *The Church on the Other Side: Exploring the Radical Future of the Local Congregation* (Grand Rapids, MI: Zondervan, 2000); Doug Pagitt, *The Emerging Church and Embodied Theology* (Grand Rapids, MI: Zondervan, 2007).

5. Some of the "emergent cohorts" founded through Emergent Village (www.emergentvillage.com), for example, meet in pubs. Perhaps the most famous example is Peter Rollins's Ikon group (www.ikon.org.uk). Other groups are meeting in homes, office buildings, and parks. Leaders are also transforming the traditional roles of pastor or priest. They tend to function as hosts who draw people together for fellowship and discussion, doing their teaching in the midst of probing dialogues about the difficulties of Christian belief and practice today.

6. John Hick, *An Interpretation of Religion* (New Haven: Yale University Press, 1989).

7. "Therefore I tell you, do not worry about your life, what you will eat or what you will drink, or about your body, what you will wear" (Matthew 6:25); "Are not five sparrows sold for two pennies? Yet not one of them is forgotten in God's sight. But even the hairs of your head are all counted. Do not be afraid; you are of more value than many sparrows" (Luke 12:6–7); "Peace I leave with you; my peace I give to you. I do not give to you as the world gives. Do not let your hearts be troubled, and do not let them be afraid" (John 14:27); "I have said this to you, so that in me you may have peace. In the world you face persecution. But take courage; I have conquered the world!" (John 16:33, all NRSV).

8. Excerpts from John Cobb's speech are quoted in Clayton, *Transforming Christian Theology*; this text is from p. 153.

9. Peter Berger, *The Sacred Canopy: Elements of a Sociological Theory of Religion* (New York: Anchor Books, 1990).

10. T. S. Eliot, "Journey of the Magi," in Eliot, *Collected Poems, 1909–1962* (London: Faber, 1974).

Index